SOMETIMES DECEIVED

how *evolutionists* have led us astray

Daniel Howell

Blue Ridge Books, LLC

Blue Ridge Books, LLC
PO Box 4623 Lynchburg, VA

Howell, Daniel
Sometimes deceived: how evolutionists have led us astray / Daniel Howell

ISBN 978-0-9987481-7-7
1. Evolution 2. Creation

213 – dc22   2017
Library of Congress Control Number: 2017937868

Project Credits
Copy Editor: Angela Teter
Original Illustrations: Daniel Howell
Indexer: Megan Boyer

Printed in the United States of America

9 8 7 6 5 4 3 2 1   First Edition   10 11 12 13 14

Dedication

To those who are being transformed by the renewing of their minds, who would not have blind faith but eyes to see and ears to hear.

Acknowledgements

Writing a book takes the effort of many people beyond the author. I would like to thank my students at Liberty University for inspiring me. Several of them read the early manuscripts and gave invaluable feedback. I especially want to thank my wife, Carla, and my children for tolerating my quirky obsessions, one of which is the evolution / creation debate. I want to thank my parents for *always* believing in me and for instilling in me a love for learning and a love for the Lord. Finally, I want to thank God for letting this book be a small part of his creation. I pray he thinks *It is good.*

About the Cover

The cover depicts a gorilla with human eyes. The blue iris and highly visible white sclera ("white of the eye") are never found in apes and give the gorilla a distinctly human appearance. The cover was inspired by a similar *TIME* magazine cover featured on July 23, 2001 (vol. 158 no. 3) with the caption *How Apes Became Human.*

Figures & Tables

Contents

Introduction

"The first to plead his case seems right, until another comes to question him."
Proverbs 18:17

How did we get here? How did the universe begin and life on Earth get started? What really happened *In the Beginning*? Everyone has pondered this at some point in their lives. Some people have devoted their entire lives to answering this question. Charles Darwin was one of those people. So was the late astronomer Carl Sagan, who explored the question more than a century after Darwin. Sagan popularized a common sentiment among scientists: *Extraordinary claims require extraordinary evidence.*

Few claims are as extraordinary as those made for the origins of our universe and life on Earth. Darwinists[1] claim, after all, that the man riding a lawn mower is actually related – genetically, ancestrally related – to the lawn he is mowing and that everything came into existence of its own accord with no plan or purpose, or has simply always existed without causation. On the other hand, creationists claim[2] there is a Creator God, one so powerful that every atom and every star sprang into being by the mere word of his mouth and that mankind was made in His image. From both camps, these are extraordinary claims, indeed.

According to evolutionists, there is a mountain of evidence in favor of biological evolution and little-to-none that favors divine creation. Is this true? In this book, we will critically examine this claim, as well as the underlying premises behind the evidence for evolution and the logic used by Darwinists to derive conclusions from that evidence. We will scrutinize the facts and assumptions undergirding the secular creation story. While I compare and contrast naturalistic evolution with divine creation, it's important to remember that creationists are religious; that is, they assert special revelation regarding their claims on origins. This is not to say they are wrong, and if they are right there should be ample evidence in favor of their position. But Darwinists are scientists making, they say, a scientific claim and so they shoulder the burden of providing verifiable evidence for that claim. Do they? Or is their mountain of evidence a mere molehill?

I said that Darwinists are scientists. Certainly, not all Darwinists are scientists and not all scientists are Darwinists.[3] A good many scientists, biologists included, are fervent creationists. Millions of people from all walks of life are creationists. Lawyers, plumbers, teachers, secretaries, electricians – lots of people reject Darwinism in favor of creationism. How is this possible? Does this mean that millions of intelligent people – including some scientists – reject science to cling to a religion? No creationist I know rejects Einstein's theory of relativity or Kepler's laws of planetary motion, so why do they reject Darwin and his theory but not Einstein, Kepler, or a hundred other scientists and their theories? Is this a clue that there's something more to Darwinism than mere science?

Is it to be taken that creationism is *de facto* false because it is popular among religious people who believe in a Creator God? Or is biological evolution automatically correct because it is purported to be science by the experts who should know (or perhaps, should know better)? These are important questions and if you are unsure what to make of the answers, you are not alone.

If you were to randomly ask people on the street to sum up the difference between creationism and evolution, they would probably say something like, "Evolution is science and creationism is religion." This answer would not reflect an uninformed opinion. In fact, it has been formed by the teachers, scientists, judges and other experts we rely on to help us shape our informed opinions. We are right to rely on experts to guide us, but doing so unfortunately comes with a risk. The title of this book is taken from a quote by C.S. Lewis:

> *"Few of us have followed the reasoning on which even ten percent of the truths we believe are based. We accept them on authority from the experts and are wise to do so, for though we are thereby sometimes deceived, yet we should have to live as savages if we did not."*[4]

Lewis is right. If we reject the knowledge provided to us by authority figures, we would have to give up 90% of everything we know and return to a life not much higher than the animals. He is also right that trusting others for so much of our information makes us vulnerable to deception. I am persuaded that biological evolution represents one of those occasions where the experts have led us astray and, far from protecting us from savagery, they have through their mishap brought us closer to it.

I do not believe that one's position on human origins is a make-or-break issue for Christians, i.e., that our salvation depends upon us getting this one right. However, Darwinism is undeniably a major obstacle to the gospel in modern Western society. A Pew survey[5] published in 2016 found that nearly half (49%) of American adults who left the church mention science as a factor. No doubt the science to which they refer is biological evolution. When a Christian or a church embraces evolution they inadvertently make it more difficult for others to come to the faith.

Who should read this book? Quite obviously it may be of interest to anyone pondering the question of human origins. However, I wrote it primarily for Christians who doubt the validity of biological evolution but don't know why and certainly cannot articulate a sensible defense of creationism. For them, this book is intended to be used somewhat like a textbook. For example, the headings and subheadings are numbered for quick reference. It is my hope that you will not simply read this book but study it. This book may also be useful to Christians who are sympathetic to Darwinism and don't know what the problem is. Hopefully, I can reveal it to you. Chapter 1 is written specifically for the Christian who doubts creationism. If this is *not* you, then you may safely skip to Chapter 2 and get started discovering why you are right to doubt Darwin.

---

[1] Throughout this book, I use the term *Darwinist* to refer to a person who espouses biological evolution as the source of life and its diversity on Earth and *creationist* for those who believe in a divine creation by a supreme intelligent being (God). These are used in the broadest possible terms, including all the various sub-categories of creationism and evolutionism. However, in this book I do not recognize *theistic evolution* (i.e., evolution as a creative force guided by a divine hand) as this is incompatible with Christianity for reasons explained in Chapter 1.

[2] To be precise, creationism is not a hypothesis devised by man but a revelation to man from God. Creationists see no conflict between that divine revelation and the facts revealed by Nature. Thus, creationists don't technically "claim" creationism, they accept it.

[3] A list of hundreds of scientists who are skeptical of Darwinism can be found at http://www.dissentfromdarwin.org/ [Accessed January 2017].

[4] Lewis, C.S. 1949. *The Weight of Glory and Other Addresses*. New York: The Macmillan Company.

[5] http://www.pewresearch.org/fact-tank/2016/08/24/why-americas-nones-left-religion-behind/ [Accessed January 2017].

SOMETIMES DECEIVED

1

DID GOD REALLY SAY...?

*"Our willingness to accept scientific claims that are
against common sense is the key to an understanding of the real
struggle between science and the supernatural. We take the side of science
in spite of the patent absurdity of some of its constructs, in spite of its
failure to fulfill many of its extravagant promises of health and life, in
spite of the tolerance of the scientific community for unsubstantiated just-
so stories, because we have a prior commitment, a commitment to
materialism... Moreover, that materialism is absolute, for we cannot
allow a Divine foot in the door."*
Prof. Richard Lewontin

1.1 Genesis

"Did God really say," whispered the serpent to Eve, "that you may not eat of any tree in the garden?"

This is the first recorded deception. A talking serpent in a garden luring a woman to doubt the words of God. Nothing has changed. Satan is still deceiving us. Perhaps Satan targeted Eve because she heard the command of God second-hand; it was Adam who heard the first do's and don'ts directly from the mouth of God. In a sense, we are hearing from God second-hand, as well, through a book delivered by revelation to other men (i.e., the Bible), and the book of Nature. The serpent tempted Eve to doubt God, but doubt was not her sin. Her sin was acting on those doubts in disobedience to God. It is natural to doubt and God did not forbid us from asking questions. The truth does not fear examination.

Like most people, I am interested in truth. With respect to our origins, I want to know what *really* happened from both a theological and scientific perspective. From either point of view, it appears to me that Christianity and Darwinism are mutually-exclusive, i.e., they cannot both be true. Those who insist they are compatible have likely not fully considered (or they deny) the ramifications of each idea upon the other. Before we can demonstrate that Darwinism is not compatible with Christianity, we have to lay down some ground rules: as Christians, if we accept that the Bible is the Word of God, that is, a revelation of God to mankind, then we should agree on these three points:

First, the Scriptures must be considered by the Christian to be infallible. To admit of errors is to deny both the claims of Scripture (2 Timothy 3:16, 2 Peter 1:21, 1 Corinthians 2:13) and early church leaders (e.g., Irenaeus and Clement of Rome) and to render the whole Christian enterprise unworthy of trust. We can certainly agree that millions of scrupulous readers over thousands of years have found no glaring errors that readily dismiss a faith in the Canon. The Scriptures have proven highly accurate with respect to geopolitical history, astronomy, archeology, anthropology, and until the mid-19th century, with respect to biology and earth science. The question before you now is whether or not you know and trust the Scriptures. Although we accept the inerrancy of Scripture, the Christian faith need not be blind. God invites people to test his claims (1 John 4:1, Malachi 3:10, Isaiah 1:18), which is in part what we intend to do here as we compare creationism to Darwinism.

> "Evolution is the greatest killer of belief that has ever happened on this planet because it showed that some of the best evidence for God, which was the design of animals and plants that so wonderfully match their environment, could be the result of this naturalistic, blind materialistic process of natural selection."
>
> - Jerry Coyne

Second, the plain reading of Scripture is the best and safest way to determine its meaning. God often uses unlearned men to communicate his simple truths to other unlearned men, and while complicated theories may be concocted to force agreement between Scripture and Darwinism, it is best for the Christian to trust Scripture and doubt Darwin when there are apparent conflicts. Attempting to force evolution onto the pages of Scripture forces you to abandon a plain reading of the Bible.

Third, God is always right. That said, our understanding of God's words may be far from right. If truth is what we seek, then we must always be willing to admit our own errors in judgment and be ready to let go of false beliefs. We must always be willing to ask and honestly answer: "Could I be wrong about this?" Indeed, maybe *I* am wrong about this. Perhaps evolution happens without a Divine hand or perhaps God created us using evolution as the mechanism of creation. I am persuaded that neither of these is the case, but I must be willing to change my mind if new evidence or a fresh perspective suggests I should.

So what did God really say about the beginning of the universe, the Earth, and us? Here is the text of Genesis chapter one (English Standard Version):

"In the beginning, God created the heavens and the earth. The earth was without form and void, and darkness was over the face of the deep. And the Spirit of God was hovering over the face of the waters.

"And God said, "Let there be light," and there was light. And God saw that the light was good. And God separated the light from the darkness. God called the light Day, and the darkness he called Night. And there was evening and there was morning, the first day.

"And God said, "Let there be an expanse in the midst of the waters, and let it separate the waters from the waters." And God made the expanse and separated the waters that were under the expanse from the waters that were above the expanse. And it was so. And God called the expanse Heaven. And there was evening and there was morning, the second day.

"And God said, "Let the waters under the heavens be gathered together into one place, and let the dry land appear." And it was so. God called the dry land Earth, and the waters that were gathered together he called Seas. And God saw that it was good.

"And God said, "Let the earth sprout vegetation, plants yielding seed, and fruit trees bearing fruit in which is their seed, each according to its kind, on the earth. And it was so. The earth brought forth vegetation, plants yielding seed according to their own kinds, and trees bearing fruit in which is their seed, each according to its kind. And God saw that it was good. And there was evening and there was morning, the third day.

"And God said, "Let there be lights in the expanse of the heavens to separate the day from the night. And let them be for signs and

for seasons, and for days and years, and let them be lights in the expanse of the heavens to give light upon the earth." And it was so. And God made the two great lights—the greater light to rule the day and the lesser light to rule the night—and the stars. And God set them in the expanse of the heavens to give light on the earth, to rule over the day and over the night, and to separate the light from the darkness. And God saw that it was good. And there was evening and there was morning, the fourth day.

"And God said, "Let the waters swarm with swarms of living creatures, and let birds fly above the earth across the expanse of the heavens." So God created the great sea creatures and every living creature that moves, with which the waters swarm, according to their kinds, and every winged bird according to its kind. And God saw that it was good. And God blessed them, saying, "Be fruitful and multiply and fill the waters in the seas, and let birds multiply on the earth." And there was evening and there was morning, the fifth day.

"And God said, "Let the earth bring forth living creatures according to their kinds—livestock and creeping things and beasts of the earth according to their kinds." And it was so. And God made the beasts of the earth according to their kinds and the livestock according to their kinds, and everything that creeps on the ground according to its kind. And God saw that it was good.

"Then God said, "Let us make man in our image, after our likeness. And let them have dominion over the fish of the sea and over the birds of the heavens and over the livestock and over all the earth and over every creeping thing that creeps on the earth."

"So God created man in his own image, in the image of God he created him; male and female he created them.

"And God blessed them. And God said to them, "Be fruitful and multiply and fill the earth and subdue it, and have dominion over the fish of the sea and over the birds of the heavens and over every living thing that moves on the earth." And God said, "Behold, I have given you every plant yielding seed that is on the face of all the earth, and every tree with seed in its fruit. You shall have them for food. And to every beast of the earth and to every bird of the heavens and to everything that creeps on the earth, everything that has the breath of life, I have given every green plant for food." And it was so. And God saw everything that he had made, and behold, it was very good. And there was evening and there was morning, the sixth day."

1.2 Is Genesis 1 Poetry?

A common argument used to persuade Christians that Darwinism is compatible with Christianity is the claim that the creation account in Genesis is poetry or metaphor and that it was never meant to be taken as literal history. Is this true? How can we know? On the one hand, Genesis 1:1 – 2:3 reads like a narrative. On the other hand, it clearly has a rhythmic pattern to it. Does it read like a narrative only because its poetic nature was lost in translation?

It's not always easy to understand a person even when speaking face-to-face. It's even more difficult to communicate by text or written word. Now imagine communicating by the written word across cultures, languages, and thousands of years of time! Although God's word is timeless and placeless, we can still misunderstand Him and what He means to say to us in the Scriptures. When it comes to rightly interpreting the Scriptures, we should keep an open mind. While the core tenets of Christianity are pretty straight-forward, many of the peripheral doctrines and truths can be obscure. Whenever possible, biblical scholars compare Scripture with Scripture rather than relying on a single verse or passage (which might be mistakenly taken out of context or simply misinterpreted).

Examine the text message in Figure 1-1. God's description of creation is in written form penned thousands of years ago in a foreign tongue. Like the mother in the text message, how can we be sure we haven't misunderstood something, or misinterpreted God's intended meaning? Can we know, for example, whether Genesis 1 is meant to be taken literally or if it's meant to be metaphor or poetry?

There are good reasons to believe that the creation account described in Genesis is meant to be taken literally. First, the Jewish work week was based on the creation events. In Exodus 20:11 we read: "For in six days the Lord made the heavens and the Earth, the sea and all that is in them, and rested on the seventh day; therefore, the Lord blessed the Sabbath day and made it holy." Second, Jesus referred to Adam and Eve as real people and the creation events as actual history (Mark 10:6, Luke 11:50-51). Third, an in-depth study of Genesis 1-11 (described below) offers a rather convincing proof that the text is meant to be taken as a straight-forward account of historical events. That is, the creation story in Genesis is very likely not poetry or metaphor but is a declarative testimony.

As it turns out, the Hebrew language uses different types of verbs for poetry than for declarative statements. Hebrew scholar Steven Boyd compared the usage of these verb types in what are clearly narrative and poetic passages of Scripture.[6] Because several events in Scripture are described both declaratively and poetically, passages even describing the same event can be compared. For example, Exodus 14 describes narratively the historical exodus of the Israelites from Egypt while Exodus 15 describes the event in a song. Boyd analyzed a total of 97 passages (48 narrative, 49 poetic). The narrative passages are heavily populated with what are called preterite verbs but possess few finite verbs. The verb usage is reversed in poetic passages. Thus, the ratio of preterite-to-finite verbs can be used to predict whether a given Hebrew writing is narrative or poetry.

Where does the creation story of Genesis 1:1 – 2:3 stand with respect to verb usage? As can be seen in Figure 1-2[7], the creation account in Genesis is unambiguously narrative. Does this prove creationism is true? No, but it demonstrates that the author of Genesis 1 likely intended for his readers to take the writing as a narrative, not poetry.

Figure 1-1: Miscommunication.

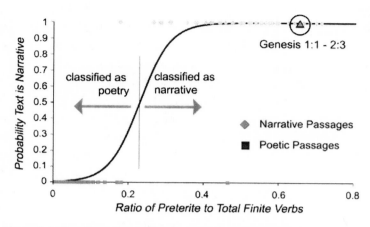

Figure 1-2: The Genesis creation story is narrative not poetry

1.3 Death

The origin and meaning of *death* as described in Scripture is absolutely incompatible with Darwin's hypothesis. This may be the greatest divide between Darwin and Jesus. Death is not a cursory subject in Scripture. Without death inhabiting its proper place even the very cross of Christ is meaningless. According to the Word of God, it was an act of man that brought death into a world previously unaware of such a thing, it was the work of Christ to defeat death, and it is the hope of prophecies yet fulfilled that a new world free of death awaits the redeemed. According to Darwin, millions of years of struggle and death preceded – even created – man.

Although many evolutionists (including theologians) have attempted to assuage the fears of doubting Christians by assuring them that biological evolution is compatible with their religion, a few leading Darwinists have been more forthright. Eugenie Scott, the founding executive director of the National Center for Science Education, a fervent evolutionist and crusader against creationism, confesses: "If Earth was ancient and populated by creatures that lived before humans, death must have preceded Adam's fall... Unquestionably, evolution has consequences for traditional Christian religion."[8]

Darwinists claim that living cells emerged from non-living materials in a primordial soup. How could this happen? What would be its driving force? And if this miracle could be achieved, why would these newly living cells, able to rise to life from the non-living, age and die? Individual cells regenerate by division and multicellular organisms are capable of replacing and refurbishing damaged and worn-out parts, so why would living cells create such self-destructive habits as aging and death?

Aging and dying are not accidents. They are not the mere wearing down of vitality, they are literally programmed into us. Any organism can be killed by another, usually for consumption or to eliminate competition, but it seems remarkably odd that cells capable of emerging from a lifeless swamp would evolve to grow old and die naturally. This is not a question that can be glibly dismissed. Aging and death are not inescapable consequences of emergent life, they developed in us presumably (from the Darwinist perspective) because they are somehow advantageous to the organism.

The Judeo-Christian God describes death as the result of sin (Genesis 2:17, Romans 6:23). Aging is merely a slow death. The process of aging for humans, and perhaps other organisms, was greatly accelerated after the global upheaval of the Great Flood. Prior to the flood, men generally lived 800-1000 years. Within a few generations after the flood our lifespan had been reduced 10-fold, as if a form of progeria had spread throughout the population.[9] This came as a proclamation from God: "My Spirit shall not abide in man forever, for he is flesh; his days shall be 120 years." (Genesis 6:3). Regardless of the pace, aging and death are hardwired into our DNA. The Christian explanation for death seems more plausible than any Darwinian scenario, but more importantly for the present discussion, the two accounts are overtly incompatible. Despite the reassuring claims of those who say otherwise, Darwinism strikes at the heart of Christianity. Nowhere is this more apparent than with the origin and meaning of death.

1.4 Delusion

The creation events described in Genesis, including the origin of death, are central tenets of Christianity, but Darwinism is formulated on the premise that there is no Creator God. Given that Darwinism and Christianity are mutually-exclusive, it is obvious that only *one* of them can be right. Some have declared Christianity, and by extension creationism, a delusion.[10] It is more likely that Darwinism is the delusion – perhaps part of the Great Delusion of the last days (2 Thessalonians 2). There are good reasons to believe the Scriptures and those reasons are the weapons we use to do battle against the principalities and powers of this age (Ephesians 6:12); they are the weapons with which we arm ourselves to defend the faith (1 Peter 3:15), which is *not* blind (Isaiah 1:18). As I've said already, God invites us to test his claims because the truth fears no examination. It is my conviction that Darwinism is a house of cards built upon wishful thinking (i.e., coherent truth) rather than reality (i.e., correspondent truth). We will examine the shaky foundations for that house beginning in chapter 2.

Romans 1:18-32 paints a vivid picture of mankind's rejection of God and the consequences of that rejection. It is so poignant and damning of Darwinian thinking that we should examine the entire passage:

> *"The wrath of God is being revealed from heaven against all the godlessness and wickedness of people who suppress the truth by their wickedness, since what may be known about God is plain to them because God has made it plain to them. For since the creation of the world God's invisible qualities – his eternal power and divine nature – have been clearly seen, being understood from what has been made, so that people are without excuse.*

> *"For although they knew God, they neither glorified him as God nor gave thanks to him, but their thinking became futile and their foolish hearts were darkened. Although they claimed to be wise, they became fools and exchanged the glory of the immortal God for images made to look like a mortal human being and birds and animals and reptiles.*

> *"Therefore, God gave them over in the sinful desires of their hearts to sexual impurity for the degrading of their bodies with one another.*

> *"They exchanged the truth about God for a lie, and worshipped and served created things rather than the Creator – who is forever praised. Amen.*

> *"Because of this, God gave them over to shameful lusts. Even their women exchanged natural sexual relations for unnatural ones. In the same way, the men also abandoned natural relations with women and were inflamed with lust for one another. Men committed shameful acts with other men and received in themselves the due penalty for their error.*

"Furthermore, just as they did not think it worthwhile to retain the knowledge of God, so God gave them over to a depraved mind, so that they do what ought not to be done. They have become filled with every kind of wickedness, evil, greed and depravity. They are full of envy, murder, strife, deceit and malice. They are gossips, slanderers, God-haters, insolent, arrogant and boastful; they invent ways of doing evil; they disobey their parents; they have no understanding, no fidelity, no love, no mercy. Although they know God's righteous decree that those who do such things deserve death, they not only continue to do these very things but also approve of those who practice them."

Almost all of the great thinkers who gave birth to modern science were deeply religious and fervent creationists. Men like Isaac Newton, Gregor Mendel, Louis Pasteur, Johann Kepler, Robert Boyle, and many more. This began to change in the 19th century. The creationist worldview held by scientists slowly gave way to an atheistic worldview, especially after Darwin's publication of *On the Origin of Species* in 1859. By the 1930s a war was raging in America's courtrooms over whether Darwin's theory should be taught to our schoolchildren. Legal skirmishes continue to this day, but by-and-large Darwinism has completely replaced creationism in our schools as it is literally illegal to oppose Darwin's view in public classrooms across America. In the 1960s, the Bible and prayer were officially banned from public schools. By 2014, some scientists (e.g., physicist Lawrence Kraus) and popular TV personalities (e.g., Bill Nye the "Science Guy"), were declaring creationism to be downright dangerous to our kids.[11] In 2015, atheist Richard Dawkins suggested that government should protect children from their religious parents.[12]

In June of 2015, the Supreme Court of the United States (SCOTUS) determined that homosexual marriage was a newfound right (*Obergefell v. Hodges*). But what does *that* have to do with anything? What does homosexuality have to do with creationism? As disconnected as they appear, Scripture reveals a relationship between our view of God as Creator and our acceptance of homosexuality:

"Because of this, God gave them over to shameful lusts. Even their women exchanged natural sexual relations for unnatural ones. In the same way, the men also abandoned natural relations with

women and were inflamed with lust for one another. Men committed shameful acts with other men." (Romans 1:26-27a).

When I was growing up in the 1970s and 80s, any kid in my school who announced he was gay would have been socially rejected and very likely beaten (I condemn those actions as most un-Christlike). That was when homosexuality was still officially classified by the American Psychological Association as a mental disorder. As I write this many years later, with my own children now in high school, homosexuality is not only tolerated in schools (and Hollywood), it is celebrated. Homosexuals rightly claimed abuse and discrimination several decades ago and all they wanted, they said, was to be treated equally under the law. But over the years they repeatedly moved their goalpost. Today, homosexuality is not to be merely tolerated by those who disagree; no one is allowed to officially reject it. It is to be accepted and embraced by everyone. Through the power of political correctness, dissent is not an option. In other words, the shoe is now on the other foot and it is the homosexuals who are the intolerant bullies. If the proof isn't in the pudding, it *is* in the cake. In 2015, two Christian bakers paid over $133,000 by court order to a lesbian couple after refusing to bake their wedding cake. They were forced to close their business. A county clerk in Kentucky, Kim Davis, was jailed for refusing to sign her name, due to her deeply held religious beliefs, to a homosexual marriage certificate following the *Obergefell* ruling. The owners of UrLoved Photography were forced to participate in sinful unions or close shop. They closed shop.

"Evolution is promoted by its practitioners as more than mere science. Evolution is promulgated as an ideology, a secular religion – a full-fledged alternative to Christianity, with meaning and morality. I am an ardent evolutionist and an ex-Christian, but I must admit that in this one complaint the literalists are absolutely right. Evolution is a religion. This was true of evolution in the beginning, and it is true of evolution still today."
- Michael Ruse, Professor of Philosophy, Florida State University

Thus, with Romans 1 as our guide, it seems not coincidental that SCOTUS recognized homosexual marriage as a newfound right roughly two generations after legitimizing Darwinism at the expense of creationism and roughly one generation after completely ejecting Scripture and prayer from our schools. It is actually nothing short of miraculous that so many Americans still believe in creationism[13] considering the almost 100-year battle for the minds of our children. Nonetheless, evolution is now the origins story believed by most of the public and its influence continues to spread. Clearly, this is not merely an academic problem. America is replacing her theistic worldview with an atheistic one and, as we read in Romans 1, this leaves us with depraved minds.[14] It's obvious that each generation is becoming more degenerate.

1.5 Science from a Christian Perspective

I opened this chapter with a quote from Professor Richard Lewontin. Here it is again, except modified as I would say it as a Christian, a scientist, and a creationist:

> *"Our willingness to accept scientific claims that are against common sense is the key to understanding the real struggle between science and the ~~supernatural~~ apparently obvious. We take the side of science in spite of the patent absurdity of some of its constructs, ~~in spite of its failure~~ because of its ability to fulfill many of its extravagant promises of health and life, ~~in spite of the tolerance of the scientific community for~~ We do not tolerate unsubstantiated just-so stories, because we have a prior commitment, a commitment to ~~materialism~~ truth. Moreover, that ~~materialism~~ commitment is absolute, for we cannot allow a ~~Divine~~ foot of mysticism in the door."*

Who would *not* be on the side of science? The problem is not that Christians and creationists have rejected science, the problem is that creationists and evolutionists now disagree on what *is* science. From my perspective, it appears that Darwinists have abandoned the scientific method to retain an ideology despite their claims to the contrary, as illustrated by Professor Lewontin's own admission. As we shall see, Darwinism is akin to religion, but evolutionists insist it is science and demand its acceptance as such by everyone. They even demand that only their "science" be taught to our children, and they have been very persuasive in both the court of law and the court of public opinion. So then we need to know: What is science and how is it performed, especially with respect to origins? What are scientific facts and how do we acquire them?

Let's find out.

---

[6] Boyd, S. W. 2004. <u>The Biblical Hebrew Creation Account: New Numbers Tell the Story</u>. *Acts & Facts*. 33 (11).

[7] Ibid., adapted.

[8] Scott, Eugenie C. 2004. *Evolution vs Creationism: An Introduction*. University of California Press.

[9] Progeria is a genetic disorder that causes those afflicted to age rapidly, a 10-year old boy, for example, having the wrinkles, arthritis, and balding of an 80-year old.

[10] Dawkins, R. 2008. *The God Delusion*. Mariner Books.

[11] https://www.youtube.com/watch?v=UTedvV6oZjo [Accessed January 2017].

[12] http://www.independent.co.uk/news/people/richard-dawkins-children-need-to-be-protected-from-religious-parents-10071712.html [Accessed January 2017].

[13] According to a 2014 Gallup poll, 4 out of 10 Americans (42%) believe in divine creation. http://www.gallup.com/poll/170822/believe-creationist-view-human-origins.aspx [Accessed January 2017].

[14] Also of note, in 1973, the Supreme Court of the United States (SCOTUS) declared abortion legal in all 50 States and unborn babies by the millions have been legally slaughtered by their mothers since; this demonstrates a general devaluing of human life consistent with the Darwinian worldview.

2

DEFINITIONS & FIRST PRINCIPLES

"What is truth?"
Pontius Pilate

Before we can intelligently discuss creationism and Darwinism we must first define some terms. The lack of clear definitions is a major contributor to the confusion felt on both sides of the origins question. We can go a long way in our search for understanding by simply clearing up ambiguous terminology.

2.1 What is Science?

Science is a search for truth about the universe in which we live. The empirical scientific method has proven to be a reliable way of increasing our knowledge of how the universe really works, as evidenced by our ever-expanding mastery of many natural phenomena. The empirical scientific method was formulated by early scientists like Galileo (1564-1642) and Kepler (1571-1630), but one of the first written descriptions of the method is provided by Isaac Newton (1643-1727) in his book *Optics*:

> *"As in mathematics, so in natural philosophy the investigation of difficult things by the method of analysis ought ever to precede the method of composition. This analysis consists of making experiments and observations, and in drawing general conclusions from them by induction...by this way of analysis we may proceed from compounds to ingredients, and from motions to the forces producing them; and in general from effects to their causes, and from particular causes to more general ones till the argument end in the most general."*

In other words, initial observations of the world help us form hypotheses which are then tested by experiment, the results of which refine our hypotheses and future experiments until we figure out precisely what causes what to happen. Newton mentioned induction. We will examine inductive and deductive reasoning in chapter 3, but as Newton pointed out, empirical scientific investigation is largely an inductive enterprise. And, as I've said, the process has worked extremely well for unlocking many of the secrets of the universe.

Clearly, the empirical scientific method has helped us to understand Nature, but can it help us to understand the origin of Nature? Darwinists claim an affirmative answer in evolution (biological and otherwise). However, Darwinists restrict their search to natural causes, *a priori* excluding the supernatural and the very existence of God. But let us suppose, hypothetically speaking, that there really is a Creator behind it all. Would their scientific approach be able to lead us to that conclusion? Would *any* truly scientific approach be able to lead us to that conclusion? What would the investigation and the results look like? If that conclusion is theoretically possible but science is incapable of getting us there, might there be something wrong with our science? If you dismiss *a priori* a possible solution to a mystery, might that affect the way you gather and interpret your evidence?

Can science help us to understand the origin of Nature? Creationists give an affirmative answer, too, claiming the data – rightly interpreted – strongly points to a Creator. There is nothing wrong with our science, at least not as Newton described it. However, many creationists believe that in recent times, in a purposeful effort to delegitimize creation-oriented research, Darwinists have amended the working definition of science to include both methodological and philosophical naturalism. Darwinists also ignore an entirely different mode of science called historical science, to be described shortly.

Naturalism limits scientific conclusions to natural causes. This limitation is logical enough for empirical studies in a laboratory or other controlled conditions, but it unduly restricts possible causes for origins. *If* it just happens to be true that the universe was created by an intelligent Being, that Being created not only the material stuff of the cosmos but also the rules for how that stuff interacts, i.e., the laws of Nature. If you accept that the universe had a beginning, the creation of both matter and the laws of Nature must necessarily have occurred *outside* those material entities and laws, i.e., supernaturally, and this may in fact be the first argument for special creation. In any case, rejecting that possibility and restricting the search to naturalistic causes means that science can never take us to the true conclusion (if there is a Creator). Science thus becomes no longer a search for truth but a means for propaganda. If, on the other hand, there is no Creator behind it all, it seems to me that expanding our search to include the possibility for intelligent causation will not significantly impede discovering the truth that there is no intelligent causation.

2.1.1 Science vs Pseudoscience

Creationism and Intelligent Design (ID) are often called pseudosciences by evolutionists. What is pseudoscience and how does one distinguish pseudoscience from empirical science? Karl Popper (1902-1994) was a philosopher of science and one of the first to try to pin down the differences between genuine science and pseudoscience. To Popper, it all came down to falsifiability. Indeed, Popper even rejected the "classical inductivist views on the scientific method in favor of empirical falsification."[15] His view of real science is basically a subtle reframing of the scientific method described by Newton, placing the emphasis on empirical results rather than the inductive reasoning. (Empirical, by the way, is defined as *derived from observation or experiment, rather than theory or pure logic*). Popper emphasized that a scientific theory can never be proved true but can be conclusively rejected by falsification. Furthermore, when falsifying evidence is found, no attempt should be made to evade the results. Instead, the hypothesis should be modified to accommodate the results. In contrast to genuine science, pseudoscience cannot be falsified either in principle or in practice by a refusal to try. That is, one is engaged in pseudoscience if their beliefs cannot be falsified, or no attempt is made to falsify a hypothesis, or a hypothesis is protected from falsification.

Science philosopher Janet Stemwedel, a blog writer for Scientific American, recently mused on Karl Popper's efforts to find the distinction between science and pseudoscience. She wrote:

> *"Popper has this picture of the scientific attitude that involves taking risks: making bold claims, then gathering all the evidence you*

can think of that might knock them down. If they stand up to your attempts to falsify them, the claims are still in play. But, you keep that hard-headed attitude and keep your eyes open for further evidence that could falsify the claims. If you decide not to watch for such evidence – deciding in effect, that because the claim hasn't been falsified in however many attempts you've made to falsify it, it must be true – you've crossed the line to pseudoscience."[16]

Thus, the goal of a true scientist is to disprove – not defend – his own hypothesis. As long as every attempt to discredit the hypothesis fails, it remains valid (or, provisionally corroborated). But does this describe the current state of affairs among Darwinists today? All of the major proponents of biological evolution say the theory is no longer questioned, only the details. Neil Shubin states it bluntly in his book *Your Inner Fish*: "Our fish-to-human framework is so strongly supported," he writes, "that we know longer try to marshal evidence for it."[17] Many universities have an Evolutionary Biology Department. When universities name departments after a theory, that theory is not open to falsification. No other theory is treated this way. There are Physics departments but no Relativity Theory departments. There are Chemistry departments but no Valence Bond departments.

As we shall see, most evidence for evolution merely reaffirms the hypothesis rather than testing and confirming it. Evolutionists are usually looking at data – be it DNA sequences or fossils – and then trying to surmise how the data is explained evolutionarily. This is not the scientific method at work. The highly-awarded Darwinist philosopher Francisco J. Ayala condemned this kind of "science" in the Proceedings of the National Academy of Sciences:

> "If a hypothesis is formulated to account for some known phenomena, these phenomena may provide credibility to the hypothesis, but by themselves do not amount to a genuine empirical test of it for the purpose of validating it."[18]

Rather than just fitting observations (such as DNA sequences, fossil discoveries, etc.) into the theory of evolution, Darwinists need to formulate hypotheses that can be put to the test. Of course, the same complaint can be levied against creationists who hold an unwavering commitment to special creation and try to fit observations into their belief system. But again,

23

creationists base their beliefs on a divine revelation (the Bible) and do not feel compelled to defend them scientifically. (This is largely what separates creationism from Intelligent Design; proponents of Intelligent Design claim only to follow the evidence wherever it leads without a prior commitment to a Creator God). If the adherents of either hypothesis spend more time defending or accommodating a prior commitment rather than attempting to disprove their ideas, then according to Karl Popper they are guilty of engaging in pseudoscience. By this definition, both Darwinists and creationists provide textbook examples of pseudoscience.

Nevertheless, is Neil Shubin completely wrong? Surely there comes a point when we have enough confidence in a hypothesis to stop searching for supporting data, right? Not really. We can have enough confidence in the results of an experiment to stop repeating it, but we should always be refining our hypotheses, especially with an eye for disconfirming evidence. Such evidence is plentiful for biological evolution but is overlooked by evolutionists or distorted to accommodate their views.

Evolutionists claim there is a mountain of evidence in favor of evolution and none for divine creation. This is simply not true. Data is data. But whether data is evidence for evolution or creation is a matter of interpretation. Both Darwinists and creationists have the same data before them, but creationists and evolutionists often interpret that data differently based on philosophical differences that frankly have little to do with science. Evolutionists interpret the data in favor of their view, and creationists interpret the data in favor of their view.

Strictly speaking, *pseudoscience* is a distorted methodology, not a topic. A scientist defending relativity theory would be engaged in pseudoscience if he was protecting the theory from falsification rather than testing it, but relativity itself would not be a pseudoscience; it is a hypothesis. Likewise, creationism is not a pseudoscience. Creationism and biological evolution are competing hypotheses concerning the origin of life on Earth. Protecting either hypothesis from falsification would be engaging in pseudoscience. Nevertheless, most evolutionists consider creationism "a pseudoscience" and vehemently denounce creation science and Intelligent Design theory as oxymorons. Accordingly, they deny that creationism or ID can even be tested scientifically. They have managed to convince most of the public, including

24

the courts, of this position. For example, in *Scientists Confront Intelligent Design and Creationism*, G. Brent Dalrymple explains:

> *"Revealed truths and the interpretation of scientific data to fit conclusions reached beforehand are not the methods of science. Thus, "scientific creationism" is not science but is religion pure and simple − a fact also recognized by federal court rulings in both Arkansas (McClean v Arkansas, 1982) and Louisiana (Aguillard v Treen, 1985)."*[19]

Of course, Dalrymple is right, but he is only half right. Both Darwinists and creationists have taken to fitting observations into their pet theories rather than testing them critically. As hypotheses, both evolution and creationism can be tested scientifically, but you must be careful to delineate between historical and empirical research in the process. Darwinists who declare creationism a religion "pure and simple" declare creationism to be untestable (as if religious beliefs can't be tested anyway). On the other hand, evolutionists have claimed that creationism is "demonstrably wrong"[20] and "provably wrong."[21] So we may legitimately ask: Is creationism a testable hypothesis or not? I guess the answer depends on what is most useful to Darwinists at the moment.

2.1.2 Empirical vs Historical Science

Time is a mysterious thing. As creatures who live in a temporal universe we divide time into three components − the past, the present, and the future. The future is yet to happen and, for all we know, may never arrive. The past is gone and the events of the past exist only in our memories or reconstructions of it. No objects exist in the past or the future. All we really have, all that materially exists, exists only in this thin slice of time called the present. All the physical objects of the universe exist only in the present. All the energy of the cosmos vibrates only in the present.

Predicting the future is virtually impossible. Even highly repetitious events, like the passing of Mars through its orbit, can only be tentatively predicted. An astronomer in 2017 may attempt to predict exactly where Mars will be on June 10, 2033, for example, only to discover that an unforeseen asteroid knocked the Warrior Planet from his orbit in 2031. Predicting the future falls into the realm of prophecy and, short of divine revelation, usually ends with failure for all but the most predictable of events (like planetary motion) in the relatively near future.

By contrast, the present can be described with extreme precision. With great accuracy I can pronounce the titles of the books in my study at this moment as I write this sentence. I cannot tell you what titles might be present on my shelf by the time you read this. The future is uncertain, but the present, although fleeting, can be described with brilliant precision.

Between these two extremes – the near totally unpredictable, indescribable future and the highly describable present – lies the past. The past is visible, but only dimly so. Objects that existed or events that occurred in the recent past can be fairly accurately described, being remembered in the minds of people who experienced them. In order for that information to be preserved faithfully, a record of the object or event must be created. Such a record may also serve to share that object or event with others who didn't personally experience it. This human record is often called a testimony. Without the testimony of a human witness, past objects and events may be forever lost to the dark expanse of time past, never to be known by those of us in the present. Of course, Nature herself may leave a record of past objects or events. These natural records – which exist only as objects or events in the present – are the only clues available for piecing together past events (or objects) that had no human witness. Generally, the farther into the past you peer, the fewer clues that remain to illuminate that darkness.

So, we cannot study objects or events of the future for the simple reason that they do not yet exist. The present may be studied and described with high precision. The past can only be remembered or discovered by studying present objects (and present events, which are present objects in motion). There are, understandably, two different modes of scientific inquiry for studying the present and the past. (How exciting would it be to have a third mode for studying the future?)

Objects and events occurring in the present are studied using empirical, or operational, science. The aim of empirical science is to understand the objects and mechanisms of the universe. The main question to be answered is *How?* How do plants grow? How do cells divide? How do sound waves propagate? In essence, how does the universe operate? This is the science that Newton described for us. By contrast, the method of discovering past objects and events is called historical science, or forensics.[22] The aim of historical science is to make sense of (i.e., reconstruct) past events and expose their underlying causes. Firmly understanding these two modes of scientific inquiry and being able to distinguish empirical evidence from historical evidence is absolutely crucial to the proper interpretation of origins data. Much confusion has been introduced – hopefully inadvertently – by Darwinists who fail to make the distinction between these modes of inquiry. Regrettably, the result of this confusion is to make the case for biological evolution appear much stronger than it really is.

The goals of empirical and historical sciences are different. The goal of empirical science is to understand how the universe operates in the present. The goal of historical science is to reconstruct the past. Their goals are different and, not surprisingly, their methods of inquiry are different, as well.

The development of the empirical scientific method in the past few centuries has provided us with a recipe that, if strictly followed, allows us to shine a light on the dark secrets of how the universe operates (which is why it's also called *operational science*). This recipe includes testing only one hypothesis at a time under tightly controlled conditions. Hypotheses are usually in the form of "if...then" (i.e., hypothetical) statements: If x, then y. The creative aspect of empirical science is devising a good experiment to test your hypothesis. If the results of your crafty experiment support your hypothesis, then they lend credence to it but, as Popper emphasized, can never prove your hypothesis true. On the other hand, your hypothesis can be unambiguously refuted, i.e., falsified, if the test results contradict your hypothesis. To have confidence in the results, they must be reproducible. That is, every time you perform the experiment under the same controlled conditions you must get the same outcome. If you do not, then you can't trust the results (and usually must devote copious amounts of time trying to determine *why* the results are not reproducible). By using reproducible results to devise new experiments, hypotheses can be refined over time leading us to a greater understanding of nature. Because our new understanding pertains to how the universe operates, that knowledge can often be put to practical use in ever-expanding ways called *technology*. The endless stream of new high-tech gadgets attests to the enlightening power of empirical science.

27

Historical (or forensic) science is quite different from operational science. The goal of historical science is to reconstruct a past event and understand its causes. Because what is being studied is a singular past occurrence, reproducibility is not an option. A murder investigation provides a good example. A murder can be reenacted, but it cannot be reproduced. The aim of the detective is to determine the particulars of the crime: who did it, when, where, why and how. Historical research is generally conducted with multiple, competing hypotheses under investigation at once. In our murder investigation, each suspect (and each potential motive) may be considered separate hypotheses. The investigators gather as much relevant data as possible with the hope that all of the data will support one hypothesis while simultaneously refuting the others. The hypothesis best supported by the evidence is said to be the most *robust*. This stands in stark contrast to the falsifiability of empirical science. In forensics, inference and circumstantial evidence are used heavily *in lieu* of direct observation. Since a past event cannot be reproduced, direct observation is out of the question. Consequently, it is impossible to establish conclusions without at least some uncertainty. In our murder investigation, a court of law should only find a suspect culpable when the evidence against him suggests guilt "beyond a reasonable doubt." Finally, because the scope of historical science is limited to past events and their causes, it does not inform us on general principles of nature or how nature operates. Thus, no technological gadgets emerge from historical science.

Discerning empirical research from historical research can sometimes be difficult and it is apparent, therefore, how even the experts can inadvertently confuse them – especially if they even deny the existence of historical science, as most Darwinists do! In Addition, Darwinists may argue, rightly, that evolution is not merely a study of the past because they are attempting to answer an operational question, namely, *how* do organisms change over time. But the question presumes the premise to be true (i.e., that organisms *do* change over time) when in fact it may not be. This is the first question to be settled: do in fact biological organisms change substantially (e.g., fish-to-birds) over time?

To complicate matters with respect to discerning between historical and empirical research, empirical studies – complete with their requisite controlled conditions, reproducibility, and falsifiability – can be employed in the course of historical / forensic investigations. For example, DNA from a crime scene can be analyzed in a laboratory, but the murder itself is a historical event. So it is with the evolutionary history of life. Empirical experiments can be performed in the attempt to shed light on evolutionary questions, particularly its mechanism. However, the empirical experiments always and only provide information about the here-and-now. Inferences must be made to link those results to the past. Laboratory analyses may confirm the presence of DNA from both the victim and the suspect at a crime scene, but many inferences may still be necessary respecting when and why and how the DNA got there. Notice, the evidence is not in dispute, but the meaning of the evidence – our interpretation of it – may be greatly disputed, as between prosecuting and defense attorneys at trial. Evolutionists and creationists have the same evidence before us, it is our interpretations of the evidence that differ. Our interpretations differ largely because our worldviews differ (more on that in a moment).

Questions of origin are historical by nature. Evolution is a study of the past – how, when, where, and even why hominids diverged from other primates, for example. The emergence of currently-existing species happened long ago and, according to the theory, ongoing evolution happens far too slowly for any single scientist to witness. Inferences must therefore be used *in lieu* of observation to draw evolutionary conclusions.

As stated previously, empirical studies can be used to probe historical questions and lots of empirical studies have been done to flesh out the proposed mechanisms of evolution. You might be surprised to discover, however, as I once was, that the results usually do not favor Darwin's hypothesis. The preponderance of this disconfirming evidence has been ignored or grossly misinterpreted by Darwinists to make the data fit their worldview.

Empirical (Operational) Science	Historical (Forensic) Science
One hypothesis tested at a time	Multiple hypotheses pursued at once
Tests performed under controlled conditions	Direct testing not possible
Direct observation of results	Inferred conclusions
Reproducibility required	Reproducibility impossible
Falsifiability	Robustness

Table 1: Empirical vs Historical Science

As examples: (1) The finding of soft tissue in dinosaur bones (allegedly 65 million years old) is a direct observation that has been practically ignored by evolutionists. (2) The preference for unobserved uniformitarianism over observable catastrophism reveals a bias that favors evolution. (3) The role of natural selection in creating new traits, (4) the existence of beneficial mutations, and (5) the assumption of unlimited variability within organisms are all resolutely defended by Darwinists despite overwhelming evidence that these pillars of evolution do not actually exist or function as evolutionists hope. The honest interpretation of the available evidence supports the creationists' position and leaves the hypothesis of evolution without a workable mechanism – the only part of Darwinism that can be tested empirically. The deductive conclusions of evolutionists are usually erroneous because the starting assumptions are likely – often demonstrably – false. All of these problems will be addressed in later chapters, the point now is that empirical science is based on observation and historical science is based on inference. Biological evolution is a historical problem, yet by blurring historical and empirical evidence Darwinists give the authoritative weight of empirical science to otherwise weak forensic inferences. Simultaneously, they reject or ignore direct observations that counter Darwinism. In 2010, evolutionists Jerry Fodor and Massimo Piattelli-Palmarini stated bluntly in the *New Scientist*:

> "Much of the vast neo-Darwinian literature is distressingly uncritical. The possibility that anything is seriously amiss with Darwin's account of evolution is hardly considered. Such dissent as there is often relies on theistic premises which Darwinists rightly say have no place in the evaluation of scientific theories. So onlookers are left with the impression that there is little or nothing about Darwin's theory to which a scientific naturalist could reasonably object. The methodological scepticism that characterises most areas of scientific discourse seems strikingly absent when Darwinism is the topic."[23]

Still, I suspect they don't know even the half of it. With respect to historical science, few evolutionists seem even to be aware of it and most who are dismiss it as a creationist tool. Ken Ham, founder of Answers in Genesis, eloquently explained historical science during a 2014 debate with celebrity science frontman Bill Nye "The Science Guy." Mr. Nye's response: "Mr. Ham, I learned something. Thank you."

While Nye's polite confession nicely illustrates Darwinists' ignorance of historical science, a summary of the debate by Michael Schulson of *The Daily Beast* nicely sums up their dismissal:

> *"Ham's argument, essentially, was that there are two kinds of science — observational, concerned-only-with-what-we-can-touch-and-see science... and historical science. This is bullshit, of course. We can use evidence from the present to extrapolate about the past. But it's straightforward, logical-sounding bullshit, which means it makes for good debate material."[24]*

Schulson is correct that empirical research can be employed in forensic (i.e., historical) investigations as I've described already, but using the word "extrapolate" is a bit misleading. To be clear, he should have said, "We can use evidence from the present to *infer* about the past." (By the way, extrapolation is a type of inference).[25] That is what we do and indeed that is all we *can* do, but stating it so bluntly reveals the weakness in their evidence, which apparently Schulson is unwilling to admit even to himself. On the whole, Darwinists are either ignorant of or outright reject even the notion of historical science. We are driven to conclude that this may be what leads them to reject creationism and Intelligent Design with such vitriol and to regard them as pseudosciences. It is likely near the root of the oft-repeated mantra: "Evolution is science, creationism is religion."

2.1.3 The Problem with History

The difficulties encountered by Darwinists trying to reconstruct the history of life are the same ones encountered by historians generally. "Events of the past have ceased," writes William Lane Craig in his book *Reasonable Faith*, "and things of the past no longer exist. Having slipped through our grasp, they are no longer available for direct inspection. At best, all we have of the past are the remains and memories of the past, which are in the present." Craig points out that the historian is

> *"wholly dependent on the present evidence for his reconstructions and inferences about the past. Since past events and things are forever gone, the historian has no way to check if his reconstructions correspond to reality, that is to say, are true... Old-line relativists often emphasize the contrast between history and science on this score. The scientist has the objects of his research*

right in front of him and is free to experiment repeatedly upon them in order to test his hypotheses. By contrast, the historian's objects of research no longer exist and so are not subject to either observation or experiment. Historical knowledge thus fails to measure up to the standards of objectivity set by scientific knowledge."

Though he doesn't explicitly make the distinction, Craig is comparing historical knowledge to *empirical* scientific knowledge and thereby highlighting the weaknesses of historical / forensic science compared to empirical science. A biologist attempting to reconstruct the divergence of two species millions of years ago has the same disadvantages as a historian trying to reconstruct the American revolutionary war, with the added disadvantages of no eyewitnesses or human records and a massively more expansive passage of time. Despite the claims of Darwinists, biological evolution, like all historical endeavors, fails to measure up to the standards of objectivity set by empirical science.

2.1.4 Blurring the Lines

It's unfortunately easy to blur the lines between empirical and historical science and it happens often when evolution is the subject of discussion. Evolutionists routinely equate historical scientific evidence (derived from inference) with empirical scientific evidence (derived from observation and experiment). Although I could fill this book with examples, I will provide only a small sampling of instances to demonstrate the point. Using empirical science to bolster the claims of evolutionary (i.e., historical) arguments is so common that you should train yourself to identify this form of equivocation when you come across it yourself.

Stephen Jay Gould was one of the most famous evolutionists of modern times. Deceased in 2002, Gould was perhaps the most influential paleontologist, evolutionary biologist, and historian of science in the late 20th century. Shortly before his death, Gould wrote a lengthy introduction to Carl Zimmer's book, *Evolution: The Triumph of an Idea*. In his introduction, which included several subheadings, Gould wrote a section titled "Evolution as True." There he states:

"Science, as we professionals always point out, cannot establish absolute truth; thus, our conclusions must always remain tentative. But this healthy

skepticism need not be extended to the point of nihilism, and we may surely state that some facts have been ascertained with sufficient confidence that we may designate them as "true" in any legitimate, vernacular meaning of the word. (Perhaps I cannot be absolutely certain that the earth is round rather than flat, but the roughly spherical shape of our planet has been sufficiently well verified that I need not grant the "flat earth society" a platform of equal time, or even any time at all, in my science classroom). Evolution, the basic organizing concept of all biological sciences, has been validated to an equally high degree, and may therefore be designated as true or factual."

And there he did it! Did you see? Gould blurred empirical science with historical science to bolster his claim that evolution is true. The shape of the earth is not a historical question. The shape of the earth has been *directly observed* by astronauts in space (and we've all seen the photographs) and the ability to circumnavigate the globe has been reproducibly confirmed by earth-bound travelers. By contrast, biological evolution has not, and in principle *cannot*, be directly observed because of the enormous time-scales required. The origin of the universe, the origin of the Earth, and the origin of existing biological species are historical events. Even when a historical event has witnesses, all we have in the present is the testimony of those observers and often that provides only foggy glimpses into the event; you need only sit in on a courtroom trial to convince yourself of this. Without a witness, past events become even more obscure. That obscurity only grows worse as we move farther and farther backwards in time. Consequently, the theory of evolution and its millions of years of slow change is built entirely on inferences and circumstantial evidence, as all historical theories must be by necessity, and thus has most emphatically *not* been "validated to an equally high degree" as the shape of the earth.

Jerry Coyne provides another example of conflating empirical and historical science in the book *Intelligent Thought: Science Versus the Intelligent Design Movement* (edited by John Brockman). Coyne starts by giving a quite good description of scientific theory:

> *"A scientific theory isn't just a guess or speculation. It is a convincing explanatory framework for a body of evidence about the real world. A good scientific theory makes sense of wide-ranging data that were previously unexplained. In addition, a scientific theory must make testable predictions and be vulnerable to falsification. Einstein's theory of relativity, for example, received a definitive test*

(and confirmation) by measurements of the bending of starlight by the sun during a solar eclipse."

Jerry Coyne is equating Darwin's theory of evolution to Einstein's theory of relativity, but he is comparing apples to oranges. Einstein's theory describes how the universe *operates* and made *predictions* that were testable, falsifiable, and reproducible. Einstein hypothesized that starlight is bent by the gravity of the sun. He could therefore predict that stars would appear out-of-place during a solar eclipse. By mathematical calculation he even predicted exactly where the out-of-place stars would appear during an upcoming eclipse. When a suitable eclipse finally occurred many years later, Einstein's predictions were confirmed by direct observation. Every time there's a solar eclipse his theory can be re-tested (i.e., it is reproducible). But – and here's the important point – his hypothesis could have been unambiguously disconfirmed had the starlight not been redirected by the sun according to his prediction. Einstein was taking a risk and putting his reputation on the line! Darwinists can make no such predictions using Darwin's hypothesis. Even the militant evolutionist Eugenie Scott conceded this (though putting it mildly) when she confessed: "It is difficult to precisely predict what characteristics will [change]."[26] Evolutionists surmise that organisms of the distant future will be different than today's organisms, but how exactly is impossible to know. With respect to how organisms will change, Darwinism makes no testable predictions. Consequently, this aspect of Darwinism, at least, fails to be falsifiable by experimentation and belongs to the realm of pseudoscience according to Karl Popper. Popper recognized this weakness in Darwinism. Popper also recognized that the mechanism of evolution – natural selection – could be empirically tested and often failed the test. "The theory of natural selection," said Popper, "is not only testable, but it turns out to be strictly not universally true." The years since that statement have only confirmed that it's an understatement. Despite recognizing the nature of the problem, Popper could not bring himself to relinquish evolution. "My solution," concluded Popper, "was that the doctrine of natural selection is a most successful *metaphysical* research programme." (Emphasis added).

The aim of physics is to describe how the universe operates; it is an empirical, or operational, science. Darwinists claim that Darwinism describes how the biological world operates, but it does nothing of the sort. It does not describe *how* cells transport materials through the cytoplasm; it does not describe *how* tissues heal after an injury; it does not describe *how* the brain works. It purports to describe how organisms change over time, but it resorts to story-telling with all supporting evidence being inferred. Being impotent to make testable, falsifiable, reproducible predictions, it is not an empirical scientific hypothesis. Unlike the bending of starlight, all supporting evidence for the past evolution of organisms can only be examined using the methods of historical science, like a murder investigation. Yet Coyne has equated Einstein's operational (i.e., empirical) theory of relativity to Darwin's historical one. Gould compared evolution to the shape of the Earth. In both cases, these men are using the prestige and power of empirical science to make the unobservable and untestable inferences of Darwinism appear more certain than they actually are.

In one last example, we read in the Introduction to *Scientists Confront Intelligent Design & Creationism*: "The theory of evolution is now as much in doubt in biology as quantum mechanics is in physics."[27] If by "as much in doubt as..." the author (Massimo Pigliucci) means *as accepted by scientists as*, then the author is correct. If he means *as empirically tested and confirmed as*, then the author is most emphatically wrong. Quantum mechanics, incidentally, has been tested and confirmed to an unusual and staggeringly high degree, making this comparison especially egregious.

Piecing together the past is difficult, even when the past was relatively recent. In 2014, a police officer in Ferguson, MO shot and killed a man in the street. This particular shooting created a national firestorm for months when it escalated into a racial issue (because the officer was white and the victim was black). To this day, many good people vehemently disagree about what occurred that day.

Darwinists decree with confidence that fish took their first steps onto dry land 360 million years ago, and that men and apes descended from a common ancestor that lived 6 million years ago. Do you really think we can enjoy such confidence with events of natural history millions of years ago when we can't even discern with complete accuracy what happened in human history just a few months or years ago? The human event in Ferguson, MO had eyewitnesses. Fish taking to land did not. The human event in Ferguson, MO had cell phone video recordings. The divergence of primates and humans did not. Evolutionists will claim that we can and do know with certainty that fish took to land and that humans and apes share a common ancestor. Yet, *how* do they know these things with such certainty? There were no eyewitnesses or recordings and *all* the evidence is inferred, mainly from facts that creationists find dubious (for reasons explained below).

2.1.5 Categorical / Descriptive Science

For the sake of completeness, I will mention a third type of science called Categorical, or Descriptive, Science. This mode of science does not involve testing hypotheses to discover new information but rather seeks to organize the facts before us. Taxonomy, for example, is the science of classifying organisms based on their characteristics. I teach human anatomy and physiology. Anatomy is defined by Google as "a branch of science concerned with the bodily structure of humans, animals, and other living organisms, especially as revealed by dissection and the separation of parts." As if to highlight the differences between descriptive and empirical science, Merriam-Webster defines anatomy as "the *art* of separating the parts of an organism in order to ascertain their position, relations, structure, and functions." (Emphasis added). In other words, anatomy is a descriptive (or categorical) science. On the other hand, physiology is an empirical / operational science which attempts to explain *how* the body works and is thus studied using the methods of empirical research. And it is the study of physiology that provides vaccines, therapeutic drugs, and other medical marvels.

2.2 What are Facts?

How do you know the things you know? How do you know, in fact, that something is a fact? Often, the facts we think are facts are not facts at all. By way of example, consider the following question and the usual answer I get from students:

Is it legal to drive barefoot in your State? Yes or No.

As a professor at a large university, I get to meet hundreds of new students in my classes every year from all over the United States. Every semester I poll my students with the above question and every class yields roughly the same result: 66% no (it is illegal), 33% yes (it is legal). In fact, it *is* legal to drive barefoot in all 50 states of the USA and in Washington, DC. It is a trivial fact, perhaps, but one that fully 2/3 of American young drivers get wrong.

Even after I correct them, many of them still insist that driving barefoot is illegal in *their* State, but a quick call to the Department of Motor Vehicles will prove they are wrong. My point here is to demonstrate that people very often and very strongly believe things that simply are not true and when pressed *they assume they have evidence for that belief even when they don't* ("I'm confident that a friend of a friend was once told by a cop that you can't drive barefoot," for example). As Ronald Reagan once quipped: "The trouble with [the opposition] is not that they're ignorant; it's just that they know so much that isn't so." I believe the same can be said for Darwinists.

It is important for us to recognize the source of our facts. There are only two ways of acquiring facts: personal experience (including personal observation) and authority. When you reflect on it you might be amazed at how many of our facts are obtained from some authority figure, especially "academic" facts. For instance, how do you know that all material things are made of atoms? Have you seen them? How do you know that the sun is 98 million miles away? Have you measured it yourself? How do you know who wrote the American Declaration of Independence? Did you witness George Mason pen the document?[28] How do you know that DNA is a long double-helix? Have you seen anything other than an artist's depiction or a computer rendering of the molecule? Did you calculate the position of each atom from Rosalind Franklin's famous photo 51 (as Watson and Crick did)?[29] Ask yourself *how you know* any number of things you know and you will quickly discover how much we depend on the word of others who have done the hard work of observing things firsthand. Depending on the word of others in this way is not unreasonable. As C. S. Lewis noted:

> "Authority not only combines with experience to produce the raw material, the 'facts,' but also has to be frequently used instead of reasoning itself as a method of getting conclusions. For example, few of us have followed the reasoning on which even ten percent of the truths we believe are based. We accept them on authority from the experts and are wise to do so."[30]

Belief, according to Google, is 1) an acceptance that a statement is true, and 2) trust, faith, or confidence in someone or something. Most of what we "know" is actually belief; a faith in the experts we trust. We also trust that the experts obtain their facts by direct observation and scientific experiment, but have they obtained all their facts this way? How have evolutionists acquired their facts?

2.2.1 Objective/Empirical vs Conceptual/Philosophical Facts

In his book *Worldviews: An Introduction to the History and Philosophy of Science*, Richard DeWitt describes two different types of facts: *objective / empirical facts* and *philosophical / conceptual facts*. What are the differences between these kinds of facts and how are we to distinguish them? D. Q. McInerny, in his book *Being Logical: A Guide to Good Thinking*, defines *objective* as "something made or done. It is something we respond to as having independent status all its own." A *concept*, according to Merriam-Webster, is "something conceived in the mind." Consequently, an objective fact is observation-based and paradigm-independent, while a conceptual fact exists only in the minds of people and is paradigm-dependent (see Section 2.4 for a quick review of *paradigms*).

Although an objective fact is paradigm-independent, the *interpretation* of an objective fact is still paradigm-dependent. For example, a piece of red, white and blue fabric is an objective fact, but its symbolic representation of France is a conceptual fact that exists only in the minds of those with knowledge of that nation and its flag. For a Darwinian example, a fish skeleton and a human skeleton are objective things that exist in the real world; they can be seen and touched and thus qualify as objective facts. However, the "fish-to-human framework" Neil Shubin believes in (see Section 2.2.2) is a conceptual fact. It is his interpretation of an inferred relationship between fish and humans, but that relationship is not an objective thing having "independent status all its own."

Are all relationships inferred? Yes, unless there is an eyewitness observer to testify to a relationship. For instance, a mother doesn't have to infer a relationship with her daughter because she is an eyewitness observer to the conception, pregnancy, and birth of the child. In the absence of such eyewitness knowledge, an alleged relationship has to be inferred based on a comparison of the two individuals. DNA comparison can be used to determine with near certainty the genetic relationship between a parent and child, but the genetic comparisons employed in that case are not the same as would be used to compare two species to infer an ancestral relationship.

The details are rather complicated, but when comparing two human individuals to assess a relationship scientists compare DNA markers known to exist in the human population with certain frequencies. If the child has a marker the parent lacks, a relationship can be definitively ruled out. If the child and alleged parent share, say, 15 out of 15 markers, some of which are rare, then we can say with a high degree of certainty (which is quantifiable) that they are probably related. When comparing the DNA of two species, however, such as fish and human, we are forced to compare the DNA encoding shared proteins or other large sections of DNA, looking for similarities and differences. This is conceptually identical to comparing their skeletons (or any other body parts) for similarities and differences. Comparing DNA sequences between two unrelated organisms is like comparing bones between two unrelated organisms; there will be similarities and differences, but the conclusions in both cases are rather weak inferences. They cannot have the empirical, quantifiable certainty that paternity tests have.

> "Evolution of the animal and plant world is considered by all those entitled to judgement to be a fact for which no further proof is needed."
> - R. Goldschmidt, in American Scientist (1952)

From the above discussion it should be apparent how crucial it is to distinguish between objective / empirical facts (e.g., skeletons) and conceptual / philosophical facts (e.g., an inferred relationship based on skeletons). When dissecting pro-evolution arguments, distinguishing objective / empirical facts from conceptual / philosophical facts is as important as distinguishing between empirical science and historical science. Regarding origins generally, and Darwinism more specifically, the question is this: which facts about biological origins are paradigm-independent? That is, which ones are truly objective / empirical facts and which ones are conceptual / philosophical facts?

According to McInerny, there are two types of objective facts: *things* and *events*. The thing is the more basic because events are composed of things in action. It's easy to determine an objective-thing fact because you can see it, touch it, and so on. A planet, like the aforementioned flag, is an objective-thing fact. An event is a little more difficult to confirm because all events are historical. At first glance this may not appear to be the case because some events are repetitive or ongoing; for example, the movement of a planet through its orbit. The orbit is an event because it exists solely by the movement of an objective thing (the planet). Although the motion of a planet through its orbit is ongoing, all we can observe is where the planet is now (in the present) and compare it to where it was yesterday (or last month or last year) to determine its movement. Thus, even an event which is ongoing can only be established by historical movements and is therefore a historical fact. Unlike one-time historical events (e.g., the American Civil War), we can make predictions about ongoing or repetitive events. We can predict the future location of a planet in orbit, a prediction which is testable and falsifiable by future observation.

The chain of events that took place, according to evolutionists, to produce the diversity of life on Earth today are one-time historical events – they were completed in the past. Even if evolution is ongoing, all we can do to "establish a relationship" is compare one thing with another thing. Note that the things being compared are not a thing such as a planet in motion; evolutionists are comparing two (or more) different things. Evolutionists do not look for changes in an organism over time, but many organisms (descendants) over time. We can track an individual organism over time to observe its migration, but we cannot track evolution this way. Thus, even the ongoing historical events of evolution cannot be directly observed like a planet in motion.

There are many things we can see and touch – real, objective things – but evolution is not one of them. First, evolution is a process, or event. You cannot directly see or touch processes, but they can nevertheless be real. We already considered a planet in motion, but let's take puberty as another example. When you observe a person at 13, 15, 17, and 18 years old, all you see is a teenager at various stages of maturity, yet the very real process of puberty is slowly transforming a child into an adult. Notice how we are again observing an individual over time, as we did a planet in orbit. Puberty and planetary motion are objective events, discerned by observing individual objects over time. Second, because evolutionary events are solely within the past (the events producing all current species happened long ago), they are all historical and all evidence for these supposed past events must be inferred only from the touchable, seeable things that currently exist, such as living species, fossilized bones, radioactive atoms, etc. We cannot directly observe the past. All we can observe are objects in the here-and-now. There is no experiment that can be performed to prove species A arose from species B 80 million years ago. There is no observation that can be made of seeable, touchable objects that can definitively establish that species B arose from species C 200 million years ago. Darwinists dig up a fork and later a spoon. When they recover a spork they are happy to conclude (by inference) an evolutionary lineage. They add this new "fact" to the "mountain of evidence" supporting evolution, but it is not an empirical / objective fact, it is a conceptual / philosophical fact, one that is given far too much weight solely because it so perfectly fits into their worldview. The entire history of the living world as proposed by evolutionists depends on such inferences, assumptions, and a good deal of faith. The events of evolution are thus *conceptual events* not objective events. The

> "In science, 'fact' can only mean 'confirmed to such a degree that it would be perverse to withhold provisional assent.' I suppose that apples might start to rise tomorrow, but the possibility does not merit equal time in physics classrooms."
> - Stephen Jay Gould

problem with evolution from a creationist's perspective, i.e., the reason why Darwinism is so beguiling, is that the picture it paints from these endless bits of inferences and assumptions is so vast and internally consistent (or *coherent*, to be described momentarily). For an educator it's like playing whack-a-mole; as soon as you dispel one falsehood three others are presented and untangling the muddled mass of "facts" is an arduous task.

Unlike the stories (or "scientific accounts") of unreproducible past evolutionary events, e.g., the divergence of man from other primates, the *mechanism* of evolution is an ongoing operation of the biological world (and even the non-biological world) according to Darwinists. Thus, like our planet in orbit, the mechanism of evolution employs touchable, seeable objects in operation and we can test at least some aspects of the mechanism with empirical studies and expect reproducible results. Do such studies support or refute the hypothesis of biological evolution? What empirical tests have been performed and what are the results? We'll examine a few of those in chapter 4.

At its core, biological evolution depends upon the following necessities: heritable traits, a mechanism for altering those traits, the existence of alterations that are beneficial, a mechanism for selecting the beneficial alterations, and unlimited variability. When examining these pillars of evolution, our goal is to discern objective / empirical facts from philosophical / conceptual facts, as well as to determine if the facts were obtained by empirical research or historical research, that is, whether by direct observation or inference.

> "No serious biologist today doubts the fact of evolution... We do not need a listing of evidences to demonstrate the fact of evolution any more than we need to demonstrate the existence of mountain ranges."
> - Preface to Evolution by J. Savage et al. (1965)

Finally, remember that the best evidence for verifying past events is eyewitness testimony, and yet even that is far from foolproof as we learned from Ferguson, MO. There are no eyewitnesses to evolutionary events that took millions of years to achieve millions of years ago. Notably, Christians believe that the God who inspired the Scriptures is a reliable eyewitness to the creation events described in those Scriptures. This, of course, means little to Darwinists who usually reject even the existence of God.

2.2.1.1. An Illustration of Objective & Conceptual Facts

Let us look at an illustration of these different types of facts. A mature apple tree is an objective fact. It is a thing "having independent status all its own." You can touch it, see it, and even taste its fruit in season. This apple tree is one of hundreds growing in rows on Farmer Jones' farm and so the "fact" that the apple tree was purposely planted by a human being seems apparent. This is a historical fact because it took place some time ago judging from the age of the tree. Without a witness, historical facts are always more-or-less tenuous. In this case, since the apple tree in question is on the outskirts of the orchard and not within a row, the seed may have been planted by the usual course of nature without Jones' input or willful intent. Finally, the "fact" that the orchard belongs to Farmer Jones is a conceptual fact. A man may lay claim to a piece of land, but his ownership is only true in his own mind and (hopefully) the minds of his neighbors. To make this abstraction more concrete we invented deeds which are seeable, touchable representations of ownership. While the bees pollinating the apple trees certainly recognize the objective status of the trees, they have no concept of the trees being owned by Jones. To further illustrate the paradigm-dependent nature of conceptual facts, consider that private ownership of Jones' orchard fits the paradigm of a 21st century American, but nomadic native Indians that roamed his land centuries ago may have had no such paradigm as private land ownership. Conceptual facts are always paradigm-dependent, but even the interpretation of objective facts is paradigm-dependent. By "interpretation of objective fact" I mean what is it for? What is its purpose? Or, what does it mean? The apple tree itself is an objective fact but when asked "What is it for?" most people would answer: "Producing apples to eat." However, this particular tree, being a crabapple, is used for cross-pollination, not human consumption, so our answer is incorrect. And if the bee could answer that question, it would likely have nothing to do with apples but everything to do with pollen.

2.2.2 Facts vs Reinforcement

Reinforcement of beliefs does not convert non-facts to facts (or paradigm-dependent conceptual facts to paradigm-independent objective facts). One infamous leader is famous for saying, "Make the lie big, make it simple, keep saying it, and eventually they will believe it." Unfortunately, repeating a falsehood often may dupe some people into believing it, but it will, fortunately, never make it true. In his book *Your Inner Fish*, Neil Shubin states:

> *"Our fish-to-human framework is so strongly supported that we no longer try to marshal evidence for it – doing so would be like dropping a ball 50 times to test the theory of gravity. The same holds for our biological example. You would have the same chance of seeing your ball go up the fifty-first time you dropped it as you would of finding strong evidence against these relationships."*

Karl Popper would certainly frown upon Shubin's confidence, but besides that, we have yet another example of confusing historical science with empirical science, and conceptual facts for objective facts. Shubin's analogy fails because you can actually test gravity empirically by dropping a ball 50 (or 500) times, but you cannot directly observe biological evolution even once. The fish-to-human framework is derived entirely from inference, not observation. After scrutinizing Shubin's book, I could find no hard evidence for his framework, only circumstantial evidence based largely on comparative anatomy. The reason of course is simple: the alleged evolution of fish to humans is a historical event (or series of events) that can only be studied using historical scientific methodology. That method can never produce the certainty that can be obtained by the scientific method employed in empirical / operational research (e.g., dropping a ball to observe gravity). Shubin attempts to bolster the fish-to-human claim by linking the historical science of origins to the empirical science of physics.

Shubin is no doubt surrounded by friends and colleagues that share his worldview, but hearing that the "fish-to-human framework is so strongly supported" over-and-over-and-over again is not evidence, it is *reinforcement* of a conviction already tenaciously held. So it is throughout Shubin's book. He provides nothing more than circumstantial or inferential proofs for this "so strongly supported" framework; proofs which are readily accepted by Shubin and his fellow evolutionists as solid evidence because they reinforce a belief they already hold, but the framework is a philosophical / conceptual one, not one based on objective facts. Their whole worldview is based upon a coherence theory of truth.

2.3 What is Truth?

What is truth? is a profound question. Pontius Pilot asked this question at the trial of Jesus, but there's no indication he paused for an answer. Jesus had earlier told his disciples: "I am the Way, the Truth, and the Life." (John 14:6). There are deep theological mysteries here, but just as God is love, so is he ultimate truth.

Truth is defined by Merriam-Webster as "the quality or state of being true" and *true* is defined 1) as "being in accordance with the actual state of affairs" and 2) as "consistent." Those two definitions of *true* lie at the heart of two theories of truth.

2.3.1 The Correspondence & Coherence Theories of Truth
There are two basic theories of truth: the correspondence theory and the coherence theory. The two theories are not mutually exclusive. Indeed, the

coherence theory is dependent upon the correspondence theory, which is therefore the more basic of the two theories. We all employ both theories every day in our attempts to discern truth from falsehood.

The correspondence theory of truth asserts that a statement is true if it corresponds to reality, i.e., to objective-thing facts. Recall that an objective thing is something that can be felt, or seen, or otherwise experienced in the real world.

The coherence theory of truth is aptly described by D. Q. McInerny in his book *Being Logical: A Guide to Good Thinking*. McInerny writes: "The coherence theory of truth maintains that any given statement is true if it harmoniously fits into (is coherent with) an already established theory or system of thought." Darwinism and creationism can be described as two views of the same photograph, one a positive and the other the negative (Figure 2-1). In both views the facts – the details of the image – are internally coherent. Jerry Coyne thinks Darwinism is a good scientific theory because it "makes sense of wide-ranging data." In my judgment, however, the Design argument is not only internally coherent making sense of wide-ranging data, but also corresponds with reality, whereas Darwin's theory does not. The facts of evolution are philosophical / conceptual facts which, although highly coherent (like the negative of a photograph), are not correspondent with objective, paradigm-independent facts, or reality (like the positive of a photograph).

Quite obviously, a belief may be held that does not correspond with reality and thus is false. Nonetheless, according to the coherence theory of truth, such a belief may be considered true by a person if it is harmonious with their worldview (i.e., their established system of thought). The false belief can even become a core belief in their worldview. When facts are presented to this person that correspond to reality but contradict their core belief, the person may experience *cognitive dissonance*.

Cognitive dissonance was first described by philosopher Leon Festinger but is explained succinctly by Frantz Fanon as follows:

> *"Sometimes people hold a core belief that is very strong. When they are presented with evidence that works against that belief, the new evidence cannot be accepted. It would create a feeling that*

is extremely uncomfortable, called cognitive dissonance. And because it is so important to protect the core belief, they will rationalize, ignore, and even deny anything that doesn't fit in with the core belief."

Darwinists accuse creationists of engaging in these sorts of mental acrobatics, and perhaps we do, but evolutionists are at least as guilty. We all attempt to organize the facts before us to fit our worldviews.

So, of course, both creationists and evolutionists can feel cognitive dissonance, but the feeling must be overcome if the truth is to be discovered. If you only want to preserve your current worldview, then by all means "rationalize, ignore, and even deny" the most uncomfortable facts. But if truth is what you seek, you must face the facts head on.

Darwinists are deeply invested in their belief system and can experience cognitive dissonance when presented with disconfirming evidence (or unbelievers). This is likely what motivates the not-so-infrequent condescending and vicious attacks on "evolution deniers." Ironically, they observe – or think they observe – cognitive dissonance in creationists:

"One explanation of how creation scientists can maintain their arguments in the face of repeated forceful rebuttals is that they are so deeply committed to their literal belief in Scripture that their interpretation of the world – their acceptance of what is real and what is

Positive Photograph | Negative Photograph

Figure 2-1: A positive vs negative photograph

unreal – is driven by a need to maintain this belief system. An understanding of this can be gained from exploring the concept of "cognitive dissonance" – a term that refers to the phenomenon whereby disconfirmation of a strongly held conviction actually reinforces belief and leads to increased proselytizing activity."[31]

The preceding paragraphs reveal a most interesting conundrum: Creationists explain the Darwinist's dogged adherence to a theory allegedly inconsistent with reality as cognitive dissonance, while evolutionists explain the creationist's dogged adherence to a theory allegedly inconsistent with reality as cognitive dissonance. Apparently, we all suffer from a deplorable lack of internal intellectual consonance.

The late evolutionist Stephen Jay Gould often reminded people that the case for biological evolution was not based on a single argument, but upon a consilience of many lines of evidence.[32] This is because Darwinism is not a single belief; it is a whole set of beliefs, many of which lie near the center of the Darwinist's worldview. In other words, they are core beliefs. In my view, those core beliefs are founded on coherent truths, not correspondent truths.

A coherent truth is not automatically false, it is simply assumed to be true without empirical evidence. A belief would be considered a coherent truth if you do not have empirical data to support the belief, yet it aligns well with your other beliefs (at least some of which, we hope, are correspondent truths supported by empirical / objective facts). Empirical data may eventually be provided to support the belief, at which point it moves from being a coherent truth to a correspondent truth.

2.3.2 Observations Don't Always Lead to Correspondent Truths

The coherence theory may be considered an assumption of truth, while the correspondent theory is an empirical confirmation of truth. As such, correspondent truth is absolutely dependent on empirical data, i.e., observations of the real world. However, observations can be misinterpreted, so even empirical data may not always lead to correspondent truth. In other words, something believed to be a correspondent truth based on real-world observations may yet be false and not correspond to reality. Correspondence is a confirmation of truth only if our understanding of reality is accurate, that is, if our interpretation of observations is correct.

Aristotle believed the Earth was the center of the universe and that the sun, moon, and stars revolved around an unmoving Earth. His beliefs were based on observations that seemed to correspond with reality – the Earth doesn't feel like it's moving, there's no constant wind from the movement of the Earth, and the heavenly bodies appear to be the ones moving as they cross the sky in regular and repeating patterns. Very likely, Aristotle would have considered his views a correspondent truth based on real-world observations, not merely a coherent truth. Yet he was wrong. We now know he was wrong because we have obtained more data – more observations – that reveal a more accurate picture of reality. Our new observations not only provide a truer picture of the solar system but also explain how Aristotle's limited observations deceived him. The point is, even when we think we have solid evidence – even direct observation – for a belief (i.e., a *correspondent truth*), we might be wrong and have no way of knowing we are wrong until more data becomes available. This is precisely why many devout Christians, believing that the Scriptures are a revealed truth from God, are willing to trust the Scriptures even when they seem to contradict some apparent scientific facts. For example, young-Earth creationists believe the universe is less than 10,000 years old despite evidence consistent with a much older universe. Their skepticism can at least be defended when it's acknowledged that anyone can be misled by convincing but limited observations.

Of course, religious people are not the only ones to maintain faith in the face of apparently disconfirming evidence; scientists do it, too. Read again Professor Lewontin's quote at the start of Chapter 1. Evolutionists have largely ignored the finding of soft tissue in dinosaur bones and tolerate shoddy dating methods.[33] They refuse to accept historical science and how it affects their conclusions. Everyone must tolerate the occasional data point that doesn't fit their expectations, but when the lion share of data points contradict your belief, you either change your belief (i.e., experience a paradigm shift, described below) or avoid the conflicting evidence altogether.

Evolutionists contend they have observable evidence to support their beliefs, but I contend they do not. They have observations from which they infer conclusions coherent with their worldview but not correspondent with reality. We've seen examples of this already (Section 2.1.4) and will see more (for example, Section 3.3.1). However, inferences coherent with your current beliefs do not necessarily constitute correspondent truth. The same goes for creationists as for evolutionists.

2.3.3 Coherent Truths ≠ Empirical Facts

Coherent truths are essential to getting by in everyday living, but they cannot dispense of correspondent truths, especially in academia. Unfortunately, many academic disciplines, including some hard sciences, are falling prey to coherent truths becoming established facts and replacing empirical observations and even critical thinking. Darwinism may have been the first ideological juggernaut to bully its way into academia, but it has not been the last. In just the past few years, strongly ideological positions on climate change, radical feminism, and sexual deviancy (homosexuality, transgenderism, etc.), just to name a few, have stormed the ivory tower. Video blogger Lauren Southern provides wonderful examples from a feminism class she took at a university in 2015. Says Southern: "We're talking about patriarchy, systems of oppression, white privilege, destroying white privilege in the wage gap... all these things as if they are fact and not something to be discussed." Southern goes on to describe how questions are framed in ways that assume coherent truths are empirical facts. For example: "It's hard to question the wage gap when the question is given: 'How does the wage gap affect women's health?' It's hard to challenge the existence of white privilege or male privilege when the questions are 'How do we minimize white privilege and minimize male privilege?'"[34]

The trend to replace empirical facts with coherent truths in these various academic disciplines is disturbing to say the least.

2.3.4 Self-evident Truth

In Chapter 3 we will be introduced to logic and the rules for making logical arguments. Logical arguments begin with premises and end with conclusions. The premises may be assumed truths, or definitions, or observations. They may also be *self-evident truths* – propositions that require no proof because they are obvious to all sane and reasonable people.

The United States Declaration of Independence contains perhaps the most famous proclamation of self-evident truth: "We hold these truths to be self-evident, that all men are created equal, that they are endowed by their Creator with certain unalienable Rights, that among these are Life, Liberty and the pursuit of Happiness."

There are actually different types of self-evident truth. Simple observations, such as *snow is white,* are observationally self-evident. Similarly, if snow is white and white is not red, then *snow is not red* is logically self-evident. A statement may also be undeniably self-evident; for examples, *humans must eat*. Attempting to prove the statement false will only prove it's true.

Although it seems impossible to prove the existence of God to someone unwilling to believe, it is self-evident that God exists to any open-minded seeker. This is, at least, the position that God takes in Romans 1: "What may be known about God is plain to them because God has made it plain to them. For since the creation of the world God's invisible qualities – his eternal power and divine nature – have been clearly seen, being understood from what has been made, so that people are without excuse."

2.4 What is Worldview / Paradigm?

I've used the words *paradigm* and *worldview* several times already and these terms need to be further explored. A person's worldview, as the word suggests, is literally the way a person views the world. Also known as a *paradigm*, your worldview is the filter through which you interpret all information that comes to you. The concept of paradigms directing scientific investigation was described by Thomas Kuhn in his book, *The Structure of Scientific Revolutions*. A notable feature of paradigms is that everyone has one. Indeed, you cannot think coherently without one. According to Kuhn, paradigms can change but do not change slowly. A particular paradigm will guide your thinking until an overwhelming amount of disconfirming evidence is collected, and then the working paradigm will give way suddenly to a new one that better accommodates all the evidence. This sudden change is called a *paradigm shift*. Such a change in worldview can only occur when the evidence against your current paradigm is so great as to create a psychological crisis. Since we cannot think devoid of a worldview, all the major pieces of the old paradigm must crumble while the new ones simultaneously arise. The old woman-young woman optical illusion graphically illustrates the nature of paradigm shifts (Figure-2-2).[35]

Broadly speaking, there are potentially many worldviews espoused by humanity. It may even be argued that each individual's worldview is uniquely their own and no one else has their exact worldview because our worldview is shaped by our knowledge and experiences which can never be shared exactly by another. That said, there is sufficient overlap between the beliefs held by members of societies that worldviews are often culturally distinguished.

2.4.1 The Two Fundamental Paradigms

Despite the plurality of worldviews, there appear to be two basic, over-arching, mutually-exclusive paradigms espoused by mankind, and they have to do with God. We can call these Worldview A (atheism) and Worldview T (theism). All of the many worldviews held by individuals fall under one of these two over-arching paradigms. This concept is supported by Scripture, for example in Matthew 25 where Jesus describes the final judgment:

> *"When the Son of Man comes in his glory, and all the angels with him, then he will sit on his glorious throne. Before him will be*

Figure 2-2: Old woman / young woman optical illusion.

gathered all the nations, and he will separate people one from an-
other as a shepherd separates the sheep from the goats. And he will
place the sheep on his right, but the goats on the left."

"Then the King will say to those on his right, 'Come, you who
are blessed by my Father, inherit the kingdom prepared for you from
the foundation of the world. For I was hungry and you gave me food,
I was thirsty and you gave me drink, I was a stranger and you wel-
comed me, I was naked and you clothed me, I was sick and you
visited me. I was in prison and you came to me.' Then the righteous
will answer him, saying, 'Lord, when did we see you hungry and feed
you, or thirsty and give you drink? And when did we see you a
stranger and welcome you, or naked and clothe you? And when did
we see you sick or in prison and visit you?' And the King will answer
them, 'Truly, I say to you, as you did it to one of the least of these
my brothers, you did it to me.'

"Then he will say to those on his left, 'Depart from me, you
cursed, into the eternal fire prepared for the devil and his angels. For
I was hungry and you gave me no food, I was thirsty and you gave
me no drink, I was a stranger and you did not welcome me, I was
naked and you did not clothe me, sick and in prison and you did not
visit me.' Then they also will answer, saying, 'Lord, when did we see
you hungry or thirsty or a stranger or naked or sick or in prison, and
did not minister to you?' Then he will answer them, saying, 'Truly, I
say to you, as you did not do it to one of the least of these, you did
not do it to me.'"

You don't have to be a particularly religious person to hold paradigm T, and people who regard themselves as religious may in fact live as if there is no God because they actually espouse paradigm A. Indeed, the shocked masses banished from God's presence in the verses above corroborate this assessment. Also, just because you hold paradigm T doesn't mean you know anything about God; it simply means that your worldview includes the belief – probably as a core belief – that there is a God.

Can people with Worldview T espouse Darwinism and vice versa? Absolutely! There are millions of religious people who believe biological evolution is true, and there may even be a few atheist who reject Darwinism. However, many Christians who accept Darwinism may not in fact be follow- ers of Christ (like the "goats" in the Scriptures quoted above). It seems to me that a true Christian can only accept biological evolution if he fails to fully understand Christianity, Darwinism, or both. These Christians have unreconciled (and likely undetected) worldview conflicts, such as the origin and meaning of death. In my opinion, those Christians who adamantly believe that Darwinism is compatible with Christianity actually do harm to Christendom. Breaking free of Worldview A concepts, such as Darwinian evolution, is perhaps the meaning of Romans 12:2: "Do not conform any longer to the pattern of this world but be transformed by the renewing of your mind."

Can people move between these worldviews? Can new information lead a person to change paradigms? Again, the answer is undeniably yes. Indeed, some Christians may argue that salvation ("being born again") is in part a sudden shift from Worldview A to Worldview T. While the core belief about God may change in an instant, many peripheral beliefs may take years to realign. This is likely what the Scriptures mean when we are told to "work out our salvation with fear and trembling" (Philippians 2:12) and, again, by the reference to "transformation" in Romans 12:2.

A person can move from Worldview A to Worldview T, but can people move from Worldview T to Worldview A? This is a matter of debate among theologians. Many hold the *once saved always saved* philosophy because Jesus said no one could snatch his followers from his hand (John 10:28). However, a number of Scripture verses indicate that a person can at least throw himself from the Lord's hand. For example, Hebrews 6:4-6:

> "For it is impossible, in the case of those who have once been enlightened, who have tasted the heavenly gift, and have shared in the Holy Spirit, and have tasted the goodness of the word of God and the powers of the age to come, and then have fallen away, to restore them again to repentance, since they are crucifying once again the Son of God to their own harm and holding him up to contempt."

And 2 Peter 2:20-22:

> "For if, after they have escaped the defilements of the world through the knowledge of our Lord and Savior Jesus Christ, they are again entangled in them and overcome, the last state has become worse for them than the first. For it would have been better for them never to have known the way of righteousness than after knowing it to turn back from the holy commandment delivered to them. What

the true proverb says has happened to them: 'The dog returns to its own vomit, and the sow, after washing herself, returns to wallow in the mire.'"

I personally know people who have walked away from the Church and a belief in God. Indeed, after graduating from what would today be called a seminary, it was presumably Darwin's data collected on *The Beagle* that changed his worldview from T to A (that, and the death of his daughter for which he could never forgive God). But there is a powerful and mysterious interplay between knowledge and worldview: while new understanding can shape our worldview, our worldview most certainly shapes our understanding.

2.5 What is Myth?

Unlike the living organisms that inhabit Earth, the definition of the word *myth* is evolving. Historically, a myth has been defined as a sacred narrative explaining how the world and humanity began and is considered by believers to be genuinely true. Bruce Lincoln, author of *Theorizing Myth: Narrative, Ideology & Scholarship*, defines myth more broadly as "ideology in narrative form." In today's popular usage, however, the word *myth* is often used synonymously with *fable* – a narrative that is taken to be untrue and fanciful but proves a point. A century ago, the common understanding of myth was likely *a story about the creation of the world and cultures that is generally regarded as true.* That definition is maintained in some dictionaries. However, the word myth as used in everyday conversation today might be defined as *a story generally believed to be true but is actually false*, and in fact that is the definition found in many contemporary dictionaries. Accordingly, someone may protest, "That is not true, it's a myth." Or a corporation may spend millions of dollars to dispel a "myth" about their company or product.

In common usage, a myth may be a story believed to be true but is false, or it may in fact be true. The ambiguous nature of the contemporary word *myth* is exemplified by the popular television show Myth Busters. In the show, widely-held myths (which have nothing to do with the origin of the world or cultures or ideology) are put to the test and by the end of the show the myth is either confirmed (a story that is generally believed to be true *and it is*) or the myth is busted (a story that is generally believed to be true *but is false*). Here, I am using the traditional definition of myth: a story about the origins of mankind that is generally accepted as truth. For clarity, I will frequently use the term "creation myth" even though it is technically redundant.

Creation myths deal specifically with the origin of the world and how people came to inhabit it. Creation myths "are often set in a dim and non-specific past that historian of religion Mircea Eliade termed *in illo tempore* ('at that time')."[36] Also, all creation myths address questions "deeply meaningful to the society that shares them, *revealing their central worldview* and the framework for the self-identity of the culture and individual in a universal context."[37] (Emphasis added). Creation myths have a way of capturing both the imagination and the intellect in order to create a unifying worldview. In the words of Alister McGrath, a myth is, "in the technical sense of the word, a story about reality which both invites its imaginative embrace and communicates a conceptual framework by which other things are to be seen. The imagination embraces the narrative of the myth, but reason consequently reflects on the contents of the myth."[38]

Special creation and Darwinian evolution are the creation myths of the two over-arching and mutually-exclusive worldviews espoused by humanity. Divine creation is the creation myth of theists and Darwinian evolution is the creation myth of atheists. They both provide an imaginative story supported by facts that explain the existence of all things in a way that links our vision of the world with our intellect, or reason. The primary differences between them is that Darwinism is supported by philosophical / conceptual facts while creationism is supported by empirical / objective facts. Darwinism is true only in the weaker coherent theory of truth, while creationism is true in the stronger correspondence theory of truth. Creationism reflects reality and is true. Darwinism reflects a fantasy and is a lie. The dark and vacuous hole created by this lie is evident to those Darwinists willing to allow that what they see in the world does not correspond with the tale of Darwin. In the words of Bertrand Russell, one of the premier atheists of the 20th century:

> "I am strangely unhappy because the pattern of my life is complicated, because my nature is hopelessly complicated; a mass of contradictory impulses; and out of all this, to my intense sorrow, pain

to you must grow. The centre of me is always and eternally a terrible pain—a curious wild pain—a searching for something beyond what the world contains, something transfigured and infinite—the beatific vision—God—I do not find it, I do not think it is to be found—but the love of it is my life—it's like passionate love for a ghost. At times it fills me with rage, at times with wild despair, it is the source of gentleness and cruelty and work, it fills every passion that I have—it is the actual spring of life within me."[39]

No doubt most of us have felt Russell's angst to some more-or-less degree. C. S. Lewis felt it but drew a vastly different conclusion to it than Russell. Said Lewis: "If I find in myself a desire which nothing in this world can satisfy, the most probable explanation is that I was made for another world."[40]

Bertrand Russell was clearly a tortured soul. He saw ghostly evidence of God but could not bring himself to believe. Most atheists refuse even to see the apparition. People generally believe what they want to believe. If you want to believe in evolution (often because you *don't* want to believe in God), then the evidence for it will seem compelling. If, on the other hand, you don't want to believe in evolution (usually because of a prior religious commitment), then the evidence appears as a house of cards. But again, only one view – creation or evolution – can be true.

While Darwin apparently adopted an atheistic worldview because of the evidence he examined, a leading atheist philosopher of modern times, Antony Flew, became a believer because the scientific evidence for God grew to be undeniable to him: "It now seems to me that the findings of over 50 years of DNA research have provided materials for a new and enormously powerful argument for design," said Flew.[41]

The fact that people can move (albeit with difficulty) from one camp to the other, indeed, the fact that people either *believe in* evolution or creation, strongly suggests that there is more at play here than mere evidence. But the average person never studies Darwinism or investigates its claims. (For that matter, the average Christian never explores the deeper things of God). For sure, the average person is told what to believe about evolution by teachers, scientists, judges, etc. – or at least by those teachers, scientists, and judges with a microphone. However, there are many teachers, scientists, judges, etc. who are *not* given the microphone and so the whole story is never told to the average person. Remember, it is literally illegal to doubt Darwin in our public education system. As the old proverb declares: "The first to plead his case seems right, until another comes and questions him."[42] The first to plead his case *seems* right, but is he? Stephen J. Gould did not feel compelled to grant creationists any time at all in his classroom. I find it deeply troubling that Darwinists are so vehemently opposed to offering a microphone to anyone who opposes (or even doubts) their views. To the truly objective observer, this fact alone should sound an alarm. Why do Darwinists fear cross-examination if their theory is so secure? If Darwinism is true, wouldn't cross-examination only strengthen their case? We are driven to conclude that perhaps Darwinists silence dissenters because they fear that Darwinism cannot withstand the scrutiny.

By crafting a new creation myth for the atheists' worldview, Darwin filled the proverbial vacuum that Nature so abhors. Prior to Darwinism, atheists could reject God and the traditional creation myth, but they had no replacement. All the major religions have a creation story, but If God didn't create, where did the cosmos come from? How did life on Earth begin? Darwin supplied the answer, but his idea was nothing less than a full-frontal assault on the Judeo-Christian scientific establishment of Western civilization. Going public with his theory was so difficult for him that after writing *On the Origin of Species* he shelved the manuscript for twenty years. When he finally did publish the work, he confided in his friend, Joseph Hooker, that it was like confessing a murder. By providing a potential mechanism for evolution, Darwin completed a new creation myth for the only worldview that lacked one, an accomplishment perhaps bigger than discovering the origin of biological species. As Richard Dawkins put it, he finally allowed one to be an "intellectually fulfilled and satisfied atheist."

Well, times have changed. Today, the atheists' worldview dominates the scientific establishment and Darwin's myth is the entrenched creation story. For any reputable biologist to express doubt in the theory would be to *his* career like confessing a murder. Nevertheless, doubts arose in Darwin's day and doubts persist in ours. Those doubts exist because Darwinism, like creationism, is not science. With respect to worldviews, creationism and evolution are myths. With respect to science, they are competing hypotheses. Creationism is not religion and Darwinism is not science. This fact will always be a thorn in the side of evolutionists.

Darwinism and creationism are the creation myths of their two respective worldviews. In my experience, creationists are generally able to appreciate this truth once it is explained to them while Darwinists are almost universally unable to grasp or admit it. I've yet to meet a staunch evolutionist who accepts (or confesses) the worldview aspects of Darwinism. The inability of Darwinists to perceive the worldview nature of their beliefs has been noted by others (e.g., C. S. Lewis; see Section 3.4). Sadly, there are many Christians who fail to grasp the worldview aspects of these creation myths, as well. Once realized, however, the revelation strengthens our understanding of origins and emboldens our willingness to share and defend creationism.

2.6 What is *Evolution* Exactly?

Consider the following logical argument:

> Premise 1: Sweet things are made of sugar.
> Premise 2: Babies are sweet.
> Conclusion: Therefore, babies are made of sugar.

The conclusion from this argument is clearly false. The fallacy leading to the false conclusion is called *equivocation*, which is employing different definitions of a word in the first and second premises. Babies are sweet, but not in the same sense that sugar is sweet. Equivocation is a particular problem when discussing biological evolution because the word *evolution* is not at all precisely defined. Here are some common definitions from authoritative sources:

"In the broadest sense, evolution is merely change."
-Douglas J. Futuyma in Evolutionary Biology, Sinauer Associates (1986)

"Biological evolution ... is change in the properties of populations of organisms that transcend the lifetime of a single individual. The ontogeny of an individual is not considered evolution; individual organisms do not evolve. The changes in populations that are considered evolutionary are those that are inheritable via the genetic material from one generation to the next. Biological evolution may be slight or substantial; it embraces everything from slight changes in the proportion of different alleles within a population (such as those determining blood types) to the successive alterations that led from the earliest protoorganism to snails, bees, giraffes, and dandelions."

-Douglas J. Futuyma in Evolutionary Biology, Sinauer Associates (1986)

"Evolution can be precisely defined as any change in the frequency of alleles within a gene pool from one generation to the next."
-Helena Curtis and N. Sue Barnes, Biology, 5th ed., Worth Publishers (1989)

"Evolution is the process by which species adapt over time to their environments."
-Smithsonian Institution, Natural History Museum

"The gradual process by which the present diversity of plant and animal life arose from the earliest and most primitive organisms, which is believed to have been continuing for the past 3000 million years."
-Oxford Concise Science Dictionary

"The doctrine according to which higher forms of life have gradually arisen out of lower."
-Chambers 20th Century Dictionary

"The development of a species, organism, or organ from its original or primitive state to its present or specialized state."
-Webster's Dictionary

"A theory that the differences between modern plants and animals are because of changes that happened by a natural process over a very long time."
-Merriam-Webster Dictionary

Finally, Jerry Coyne, in his book *Why Evolution Is True* writes:

"The modern theory of evolution is easy to grasp. It can be summarized in a single (albeit slightly long) sentence: Life on earth evolved gradually beginning with one primitive species – perhaps a self-replicating molecule – that lived more than 3.5 billion years ago; it then branched out over time, throwing off many new and diverse species; and the mechanism for most (but not all) of evolutionary change is natural selection."

Most of the above definitions are as atrocious as they are varied. For instance, evolution apparently has no bearing on bacteria, protists, or fungi according to Merriam-Webster and even the Oxford Concise Science Dictionary, which also limits the processes of evolution to a specific 3-billion year period. According to Douglas Futuyma, "biological evolution may be slight or substantial." Of course, *slight* and *substantial* must now be precisely defined in this context, but they are not. Both Chambers and Webster's dictionaries explicitly codify the idea that evolution leads from primitive to advanced, a related concept generally known as *universal evolutionism* (see Section 4.1.1) which was also espoused by Charles Darwin. As for Jerry Coyne, he should know not to use the word you are defining in the definition, or that words like "perhaps" don't lend much confidence to a definition. Curiously, he considers a completely fictitious "self-replicating molecule" to be a "species," which may be possible since the word *species* is almost as hard to define as *evolution*. Finally, it should be noted that according to Chambers 20th Century dictionary, evolution is a doctrine (and, according to Google, *doctrine* is defined as "a belief or set of beliefs held and taught by a church, political party, or other group." Synonyms include creed, dogma, and ideology).

Keep in mind, the above definitions are only a sampling of the definitions offered by authoritative sources, and there are numerous more definitions offered by non-authoritative sources which influence the way people conceive of and utilize the word *evolution*. The lack of a solid definition seriously complicates any discussion or debate on the issue and equivocation runs rampant.

2.7 First Principles

First principles are foundational, self-evident propositions that cannot be deduced from other propositions or assumptions. They are the canons upon which further conclusions are derived. Several first principles are important to the study of origins.

2.7.1 The Structure-Function Principle

The Structure-Function Principle, also known as the Principle of Complementarity, states that the function of a thing is intimately related to its structure. An application of this law can be easily seen in the wheel. A wheel on a car (or train, or plane, etc.) is circular and can only be circular as this is the only structure suitable for its function, rolling a carriage. A square, triangle, or any other shape will not suffice, or will at least be inferior. Similarly, an airfoil or wing of a plane must conform to a specific shape in order to perform its function of lift. In the biological world, the lungs have particular structures for extracting oxygen from the atmosphere, gills have structures for extracting oxygen from water, hands (human, ape, or otherwise) are suitable for grasping food and other objects. A million more examples could be provided because for *every* function to be accomplished only structures of suitable *shapes* are capable.

Protein biochemists are keenly aware that a protein's function is determined by its three-dimensional shape. Even a small change in shape caused by an alteration in the protein's amino acid sequence can destroy completely the protein's function.

It is an empirical fact that the nucleotide sequence of human DNA is more similar to chimp DNA than dog DNA. It is also more similar to dog DNA than fish DNA. Why is this? Does this suggest some kind of evolutionary, ancestral relationship between these organisms? While the observation is consistent with that conclusion (which would suffice for a philosophical / conceptual fact), it is not the only explanation and may not be the most parsimonious. The similarities in DNA sequences can also be explained (and is indeed predicted) by the Structure-Function Principle. Dogs and humans share more structural similarities than humans and fish, so more similarities in DNA (which codes for those structures) are to be expected. Likewise, humans and fish share more similarities than humans and algae, so not surprisingly our DNA is more similar to fish than algae. Thus, even if DNA sequence similarities resemble an evolutionary tree, they do not demonstrate ancestral relationships. The Tree of Life could also be interpreted as a map of the Structure-Function Principle at work in the biological realm, both in genotype (i.e., gene DNA sequence) and in phenotype (i.e., structures produced by gene expression).

2.7.2 Information

People have always wondered about the fundamental components of the universe. The ancients believed everything was composed of four basic elements – earth, wind, fire, and water. While our understanding of the fundamentals has advanced beyond that simple description, we still have much to learn. You are no doubt familiar with atoms and the periodic table of the elements, and you are probably familiar with the concept of energy. For centuries we understood the universe to be composed of these two basic entities – matter and energy. Indeed, what we call the Laws of Nature worked out over the past several centuries are largely descriptions of how matter and energy interact. Though it went without notice for hundreds of years, implicit in these laws is the existence of a third fundamental entity: *information*.

Information is neither matter nor energy and yet it is as real and as necessary as the other two. Perhaps it is not surprising that humanity failed to recognize this third fundamental entity until we entered into our own Information Age. Ironically, information in nature is perhaps seen nowhere more plainly than in the realm of one of the oldest subjects of science – biology. In the last century we discovered the ultimate purveyor of information in nature: DNA (deoxyribonucleic acid). DNA is literally a cellular library, or memory stick, where the cell stores a code for the construction of cells, tissues, organs, and organisms.

Eugenie Scott, like nearly all evolutionists, still dismisses this third entity of nature completely when she starts chapter one of her book *Evolution vs Creationism* with the words: "We live in a universe made up of matter and energy, a *material* universe." (Emphasis in original). However, matter and energy mean nothing without information. There are Laws of Nature that are strictly obeyed by the matter and energy of the universe. Who wrote the laws of physics? Who decided the rules of chemistry? Who determined the speed of light, the value of the gravitational constant, or the way atoms would intermingle to form molecules? Eugenie Scott would perhaps argue that the laws of nature are emergent, arising from the physical properties of matter, but this supposition is an untestable position of faith, just as the belief that God set the speed limit of light in a vacuum at 186,282 miles per second. Even if the properties of most materials – like gold or carbon or electrons – are emergent, this doesn't resolve the fundamental problem. It seems unavoidable that at some bedrock level a material entity with certain intrinsic properties must exist such that, when interacting with itself or other materials, the emergent properties are revealed. For example, a proton has certain properties (e.g., size and charge) that are evidently emergent since the proton is made of quarks and gluons. The properties of quarks and gluons may be emergent if they are constructed of more fundamental particles, but at some point you reach the bedrock particles which do not have emergent properties, but intrinsic properties. What is the source of those particles and their intrinsic properties? Whether you believe the answer is God or Nature, either is a matter of faith. Most certainly, the coded instructions in DNA are not emergent properties of nucleotides or the atoms that compose them.

2.7.2.1 Cellular Information & Overcoming Chaos

A remarkable paper was published in 2011 by researchers Peter Tompa and George Rose in the journal *Protein Science*. By every indication, these researchers are evolutionists with no sympathy for creationism, yet, their paper makes a very strong case for the intelligent design of life. It is titled "The Levinthal Paradox of the Interactome."[43]

In the 1960s, Cyrus Levinthal made a back-of-the-envelope calculation (later published) which mathematically demonstrated that a protein could not fold into its functional shape by randomly testing every possible conformation it could physically take. The number of possible shapes is so enormous that to sample them all would require more time, even for a small protein, than the age of the universe (assuming 15 billion years for the age). Scientists have concluded that spontaneous protein folding is directed somehow and the directions are stored within the amino acid sequence of the polypeptide chain.

A cell is made of millions of molecular components – proteins, sugars, lipid membranes, DNA, chemical messengers, metabolic pathways, nutrients, ions, cofactors, etc. These components do not exist or function in isolation; rather, they work together in functional units. Just as the steering wheel, brakes, transmission, pistons, and gas tank must be properly arranged to make a functioning car, the millions of molecular components within a cell must be properly arranged in order to interact in a viable way. The sum total of this functional, dynamic arrangement of cellular parts is called the *interactome*. Unlike a car, which can be taken apart and reassembled as a functioning vehicle, the cell cannot be reassembled if the interactome disintegrates. Consequently, death is irreversible.

In their paper, Tompa and Rose extended Levinthal's calculation of the probability of a protein finding its proper form by randomly searching every possible shape to the components of the interactome finding their viable arrangement by random search of every possible way cellular components could interact with each other. In other words, using our car analogy, in how many possible ways can you arrange tires, steering wheels, radios, brakes, pistons, bumpers, etc. together? Not surprisingly, the number is staggeringly large (that is, the probability of getting them arranged right is staggeringly small). According to Tompa and Rose, the odds of all the components in a cell spontaneously arranging themselves in a manner conducive to life is just one in $10^{8 \times 10^{10}}$ (10 to the 8th times 10 to the 10th power). As the authors of the paper state bluntly, this number is "tantamount to a proof that the cell does not organize by random collisions of its interacting constituents."

Their result, of course, is not unexpected or surprising. We all know only too well that death is irreversible and that living cells only come from the division of pre-existing living cells. The mother cell provides an "interactome template" that the daughter cells inherit and maintain through the constant expenditure of energy. Of interest to the origins debate, however, are several other insights by the authors:

> *"Over and above combinatorial complexity, there is a fundamental "chicken-and-egg" dilemma: correct interpretation of assembly signals and pathways may require a prior network of interacting proteins, that is, the interactome itself. For example, mRNA localization requires the cytoskeleton, along which transport can proceed. In turn, the cytoskeleton requires prior organization, such as the microtubule-organizing centers (MTOCs), for proper assembly, and transport along the cytoskeleton requires protein motors, large complexes themselves. Again the nuclear export signal requires the presence and operation of the nuclear pore complex for proper op-*

eration. Although cellular function depends upon the "elaborate net-work of interlocking assembly lines,"[44] it cannot be established in the absence of its own prior formation, a conundrum at the crux of self-replicating life."

The above quote is a mouthful for non-biologists, but it is one of the best descriptions of irreducible complexity (see Section 4.2.1) ever made by evolutionists. The entire paper is essentially a demonstration of the correctness of Michael Behe's hypothesis, for which he has been mercilessly ridiculed. The authors continue:

"Perhaps the most profound conclusion to be drawn from our calculations... is that the emergent interactome could not have self-organized spontaneously from its isolated protein components. Rather, it attains its functional state by templating the interactome of a mother cell and maintains that state by a continuous expenditure of energy. In the absence of a prior framework of existing interactions, it is far more likely that combined cellular constituents would end up in a non-functional, aggregated state, one incompatible with life."

Now for the cognitive dissonance. Despite the fact that their conclusions firmly support the Intelligent Design hypothesis over Darwinism, Tompa and Rose affirm their commitment to evolution:

"An implicit consequence of [our research] is that life would have traversed [this lethal level of disorganization] at least once. Presumably, early-earth life forms originated through an accumulation of changes of ever increasing complexity, resulting eventually in photosynthetic prokaryotes."

In two sentences, Tompa and Rose completely dismiss the punchline of their entire paper – the *proof* they just offered that life cannot arise spontaneously – and affirm instead their *faith* that evolution accomplished the miracle somehow.

As a final thought, it's interesting that Tompa and Rose specifically mention photosynthesis in a sentence which is almost certainly meant to downplay the first cell's miraculous victory over interactome chaos. Photosynthesis is often considered the pinnacle of cellular achievements. As one science writer puts it: "The photosynthetic technique for transferring energy from one molecular system to another should make any short-list of Mother Nature's spectacular accomplishments."[45] All the more stunning that this accomplishment was evidently one of the first functional interactomes to emerge from the primordial soup.

2.7.2.2 Information & Junk DNA

DNA is the repository of information in the cell. There is roughly 1 meter of DNA packed into every cell in your body. Is all of that DNA necessary or is much of that DNA leftover evolutionary relic?

In September of 2012 a study was published on the Encyclopedia of DNA Elements (ENCODE) project probing the above question, among others. One finding of the study is that at least 80% of the human genome is active. This is extraordinarily significant since in August of 2012 virtually every biology teacher and scientist in America would have said that roughly 97% of the genome is "junk" DNA – useless remnants of a long evolutionary past of failures, false starts, and extinct genes.

The finding is also significant for what it demonstrates about origins research. Many scientists continue to claim that creationism and ID make no testable predictions. Indeed, philosopher of science Philip Kitcher called ID a "dead science" for this very reason. He, like other evolutionists, claimed that junk DNA was expected by evolution but unexplainable if humans were intelligently designed. A major reason why Kitcher rejected ID is, in fact, because it "fails to explain the facts of biology today – in particular the pervasive presence of junk DNA within our genome."

Kitcher was clearly wrong, not just about junk DNA but also about ID. Proponents of ID predicted long before ENCODE that junk DNA was not, in fact, junk. In 2005, creationist and scientist Stuart Burgess wrote:

> "Scientists used the term "junk DNA" to describe sections of the genome that did not contain genes. This term was used because it was assumed that non-gene DNA performed no functions and was just useless. However, in recent years, discoveries have been made that show that sections of so-called "junk DNA" actually perform very important functions. These functions include such things as the regulation of developmental changes in the embryo during growth and

the control of structural changes in the DNA molecule during functioning of the cell. It is likely that other sophisticated functions of "junk DNA" will be discovered in the future."[46]

In 1998, fourteen years before ENCODE, William Dembski predicted: "On an evolutionary view we expect a lot of useless DNA. If, on the other hand, organisms are designed, we expect DNA, as much as possible, to exhibit function." The results of the ENCODE project clearly support the predictions of creationists, not Darwinists. However, these results will never be acknowledged by Darwinists as a victory for creationism, neither will they be regarded as a falsification of Darwinism because Darwinism cannot be falsified.

2.7.2.3 DNA and a Broken Molecular Clock

DNA is composed of four nucleotides: thymine (T), cytosine (C), adenine (A), and guanine (G). The genetic code is created by grouping the four nucleotide "letters" into three-letter "words" (called codons). Three-letter words created with an alphabet of four letters allows 64 unique words ($4^3 = 64$). Since proteins are made from only 20 amino acids, there is more than one codon assigned to each amino acid. Having multiple codons assigned to each amino acid is called *redundancy*. As it turns out, most amino acids are encoded by just the first two letters of the codon, the third codon being unimportant due to redundancy. For example, the amino acid serine is encoded by the codons TCT, TCC, TCA, and TCG; in other words, TCx. For decades scientists assumed that redundancy acted simply as a dampener on the effects of mutations. Thus, a mutation that converts TCT to TCC still results in serine and the integrity of the protein product is preserved. That is, the third nucleotide in a codon is free to mutate without consequences to the organism. That being the case, these redundant mutations may be used to measure evolutionary time scales; for example, the time since two species diverged from a common ancestor.

Scientists frequently attempt to determine when two evolutionarily-related organisms diverged by comparing redundant mutations in their DNA. For example, suppose that a stretch of DNA found in two species differs by four base pairs and the rate of mutation is "known" to be one base per 25 million years. This would indicate a common ancestor approximately 50 million years ago (see Figure 2-3).[47] This dating technique is called the *molecular clock*. Of course, accurate dating depends on several conditions: 1) the two species are actually related ancestrally, 2) the mutation rate is accurately known, and 3) the differences between the sequences are purely the result of random mutations accumulated in redundant nucleotides. Condition #1 is impossible to confirm empirically (i.e., without inference) and condition #2 is extremely difficult, if not impossible, to determine with accuracy. Condition #3 was the one most likely to be universally accepted, but new information suggests that it may not be safe to assume condition #3 after all. A paper[48] published in 2014 reveals that what we have considered redundancy is actually a code within the genetic code and this discovery throws a major wrench into the molecular clock apparatus.

The authors of the 2014 paper demonstrate that the genetic code is not simply redundant. Instead, different codons for the same amino acid are employed to regulate the pace of translation. What have been traditionally considered redundant codons are now known to communicate different pause rates to the ribosome during translation, which allow the new protein chains time to fold properly in differing conditions For example, TCC might tell the ribosome to insert a serine and keep zipping along, whereas TCA

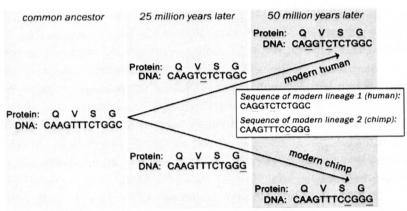

The DNA sequence may change over time without changing the sequence of the coded protein due to 'redundancy' in the genetic code.

Figure 2-3: The molecular clock.

might tell the ribosome to insert a serine and then wait 5 milliseconds before continuing. Because of this new finding we can only conclude that using DNA redundancy to determine evolutionary timescales (i.e., the molecular clock) is not valid because the sequence differences in different organisms may not be due to random mutations accumulated over time. Rather, they are purposeful differences that regulate translation. The redundant codons are not redundant; they convey distinct instructions to the protein production machinery. Remarkably, there appears to be a hierarchy of information – a code within a code – embedded within the molecule we call DNA. We may yet discover other instructions coded within DNA.

Beyond the problems with the molecular clock, take a moment to reflect on the nature of the genetic code. It is literally a *code*. Languages and codes are the products of intelligent minds. Like the codes employed by the Germans in the Second World War, the genetic code needed to be cracked and it took many scientists more than a decade to crack it. The code consists of 64 three-letter words (i.e., codons) coding for 20 amino acids with start, stop, and pause signals. This code is found in every living thing on Earth, from viruses and bacteria to plants and people. Just as we might do for any book, the DNA message is both transcribed (i.e., copied) and translated (from DNA language to protein language) inside the cell. Is this evidence of common ancestry or common design? It is objective / empirical evidence for neither, but philosophical / conceptual evidence for either. One thing is for sure: there is currently no naturalistic explanation for the origin of information or codes.

2.7.2.4 *Timing Evolution*

Even without the aforementioned problems, the molecular clock is a Darwinian timepiece in dire need of resetting. In 2004, evolutionists Dan Graur and William Martin published a paper titled "Reading the Entrails of Chickens: Molecular Timescales of Evolution and the Illusion of Precision."[49] The authors note that medieval scholars futilely attempted to date monumental past events with extremely high precision, such as James Ussher (1581-1656) who dated the first day of creation as Sunday, October 23, 4004 BC. Turning to modern scholars, they discharged a lethal shot in the introduction to their paper:

"We will relate a dating saga of ballooning inapplicability and snowballing error through which molecular equivalents of the 23rd October 4004 BC date have been mass-produced in the most prestigious biology journals."

Their paper is a scathing rebuke of the shoddy methodologies that plague evolutionary timescale measurements. However, like the paper by Tompa and Rose, Graur and William's paper has been largely ignored by their Darwinists colleagues and bogus calculations continue to be manufactured and reported.

2.7.3 The Anthropic Principle

To many millions of people, myself included, the universe appears to be designed for life, even particularly for life on Earth. It is admitted by creationists and evolutionists alike that life as we know it depends entirely on the physical constants of nature being precisely as they are. If the speed of light, the mass of a proton, the charge on an electron, the force of gravity, the freezing point of water, or any number of other physical parameters were even slightly different, life as we know it simply would not exist. If the Earth were closer to the sun, the moon larger or smaller, the sun hotter or cooler, life would not saturate this planet.

The apparent fine-tuning of our planet, solar system, and universe to meet the needs of life on Earth is called the *Anthropic Principle*. This seemingly forceful argument for design is yet rebuffed by evolutionists. Some stress that the conditions are ripe for life *as we know it*, but if the conditions or constants were different, then simply a different form of life would have emerged (in a universe apparently designed for it). That may be a reasonable hypothesis, but one that is unfortunately impossible to test. Other evolutionists concede that life might only exist in a universe like ours, but that countless universes do or have existed on the way to discovering the necessary conditions for life (see Section 5.3). Again, a hypothesis that regrettably is untestable. One evolutionist professor dismissed the anthropic principle entirely with the following classroom demonstration: With 150 students in his classroom, each student was asked to write down on a piece of paper his or her birthday. "What are the odds," asked the professor, "that we arrive at the exact combination of birthdays found in our classroom? And yet, here we are." As usual, there is a flaw in this Darwinist professor's argument. Before I expose it, can you find it? If you are a Christian desiring to defend creationism, you must become proficient at finding the flaws in Darwinists' arguments (they always have them).

The odds of arriving at the exact birthday combination are staggeringly small, $(1/365)^{150}$ to be precise (excluding leap year births). But the professor's argument contains a fatal flaw. Almost certainly a unique combination will be obtained with every class surveyed, but every possible combination is *acceptable*. That is to say, every class will have a unique and unlikely combination, but there is no penalty for getting the "wrong" combination nor any reward for getting the "right" one. Of the trillions of combinations possible for the physical constants and conditions required for life on Earth, only one – or perhaps a very small few – would reward the universe with life. And yet, here we are. The Anthropic Principle is dismissed or ignored by evolutionists, but to my mind it makes a very powerful argument for divine creation.

2.8 What is Origins?

Before leaving this chapter on definitions we should define *origins*. Origins is a branch of science, the goal of which is to discover the beginning of things, and here we are concerned mainly with the beginning of life and biological species. There are currently two proposals for biological origins: naturalistic evolution and divine creation. Evolution is composed of two parts – the mythical part and the mechanistic part. The mechanism of evolution – natural selection – can be investigated empirically, but does it pass the test? We shall see in Chapter 4.

The mythical part of evolution and the myth of divine creation cannot be studied empirically, but they can be examined using historical scientific methods. Since their conclusions are based on inferences (whose premises are knee-deep in paradigm-dependent facts and coherent truths), neither can be truly falsified. However, since evolution and creation are mutually-exclusive, only one can be right. Thus, we can ask which hypothesis is best supported by the circumstantial evidence, i.e., which one is most *robust*? Answering that question requires the use of sound logic and reason, the subject of Chapter 3.

[15] https://en.wikipedia.org/wiki/Karl_Popper [Accessed June 2015]

[16] https://blogs.scientificamerican.com/doing-good-science/drawing-the-line-between-science-and-pseudo-science/ [Accessed January 2017].

[17] Shubin, N. 2008. *Your Inner Fish: A journey into the 3.5-billion-year history of the human body*. New York: Pantheon Books, page 128

[18] Francisco J. A. 2009. Darwin and the scientific method. *Proceedings of the National Academy of Sciences* 106: 10033-10039.

[19] Petto, A.J. and L.R. Godfrey, eds. 2007. *Scientists Confront Intelligent Design and Creationism*. W.W. Norton & Company, page 152.

[20] ibid, page 151

[21] ibid, page 147

[22] Technically, forensics is a particular branch of historical science dealing with jurisprudence, particularly in criminal cases. However, because many people are already familiar with forensics and crime scene investigations, I may use the terms *historical science* and *forensics* interchangeably.

[23] https://www.newscientist.com/article/mg20527466-100-survival-of-the-fittest-theory-darwinisms-limits/ [Accessed January 2017].

[24] http://www.thedailybeast.com/articles/2014/02/05/the-bill-nye-ken-ham-debate-was-a-nightmare-for-science.html [Accessed January 2017].

[25] Extrapolation is a particular type of inferences. To extrapolate, according to Merriam-Webster, means to surmise values of a variable in an *unobserved interval* from values within an *already observed interval*. For example, you observe the sequence 2, 4, 8, 16 and by extrapolation you infer the following sequence: 32, 64, 128. Non-numerical extrapolation is also legitimate. For example, to extrapolate public sentiment on one issue based on prior public reaction to another related issue. The inferences made by Darwinists are generally *not* extrapolations. In the limited cases where extrapolation is genuinely employed, it is used erroneously, as demonstrated in Section 3.3.3.

[26] Scott, E.C. 2004. *Evolution vs Creationism: An Introduction*. Greenwood Press.

[27] Petto, A.J. and L.R. Godfrey, eds. 2007. *Scientists Confront Intelligent Design and Creationism*. W.W. Norton & Company.

[28] Yes, I know Thomas Jefferson wrote the Declaration of Independence. Did you? How did you know?

[29] Rosalind Franklin generated exceptional X-ray crystallography photographs of DNA while working in the laboratory of Maurice Wilkins at Kings College. Wilkins showed her notebooks (including the spectacular photo 51) to James Watson without Franklin's knowledge or consent. Watson

and Francis Crick subsequently deduced the structure of DNA from her data, published their seminal 1953 paper, and eventually (along with Maurice Wilkins) won the Nobel Prize without giving Franklin the credit she deserved. In 1958, Franklin died of cancer, possibly from exposure to X-rays.

[30] Lewis, C.S. 1949. *The Weight of Glory and Other Addresses.* New York: The Macmillan Company.

[31] Petto, A.J. and L.R. Godfrey, eds. 2007. *Scientists Confront Intelligent Design and Creationism.* W.W. Norton & Company.

[32] Gould, S. J. 1987. Darwinism Defined: The Difference between Fact and Theory. *Discover* 8:64-70

[33] Graur, D. and W. Martin. 2004. Reading the entrails of chickens: molecular timescales of evolution and the illusion of precision. *Trends Genetics* 20 (2):80-86.

[34] https://www.youtube.com/watch?v=JowiDnuBTHU&feature=youtu.be. [Accessed May 2016].

[35] Public domain (fair use). In case you have a hard time seeing both images in the illusion, here is the image with labels:

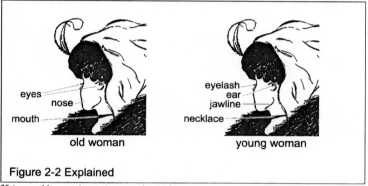

Figure 2-2 Explained

[36] http://en.wikipedia.org/wiki/Creation_myth [Accessed June 2013].

[37] Ibid.

[38] CS Lewis Symposium 1/3: Rational Argument – Alister McGRath, https://www.youtube.com/watch?v=aAJh6Z9Q3c4 [Accessed January 2017].

[39] Bertrand Russel penned these words in a letter to one of his many mistresses, Constance Malleson. Monk, R. 1996. *Bertrand Russell: The Spirit of Solitude 1872-1971.* Free Press.

[40] Lewis, C.S. 1996. *Mere Christianity.* Touchstone Books. (First published in 1952).

[41] Flew, A. and R.A. Varghese. 2007. *There is a God.* HarperOne.

[42] Proverbs 18:17

[43] Tompa, P. and G. D. Rose. 2011. The Levinthal paradox of the interactome. *Protein Science* 20 (12):2074-79.

[44] Alberts, B. 1998. The cell as a collection of protein machines: preparing the next generation of molecular biologists. *Cell* 92:291-94.

[45] Yarris, L. 2007. Quantum Secrets of Photosynthesis Revealed. *Research News*. http://www2.lbl.gov/Science-Articles/Archive/PBD-quantum-secrets.html [Accessed January 2017].

[46] Burgess, S. 2005. *The Design and Origin of Man.* Day One Publications.

[47] Adapted from http://evolution.berkeley.edu/evosite/evo101/IIE1cMolecularclocks.shtml [Last accessed 2015, no longer available].

[48] D'Onofrio, D. J. and D. L. Abel. 2014. Redundancy of the genetic code enables translational pausing. *Front. Genet.* 5:140

[49] Graur, D. and W. Martin. 2004. Reading the entrails of chickens: molecular timescales of evolution and the illusion of precision. *Trends Genetics* 20 (2):80-86.

3

LOGIC & REASON

"There are only two kinds of people; those who accept dogma and know it, and those who accept dogma and don't know it."
G.K. Chesterton

Aristotle defined man as the rational animal. In the Scriptures, God invites men to "Come, let us reason together." (Isaiah 1:18). Among all the creatures on Earth, man alone has the ability to employ logic, to reason, to think rationally. For Christians, this is an important part of what it means to be made "in the image of God." (Genesis 1:27).

Inference is a form of reasoning in which a conclusion is derived (i.e., inferred) from premises. Logic, according to the Merriam-Webster dictionary, is "a science that deals with the principles and criteria of validity of inference and demonstration: the science of the formal principles of reasoning." Understanding logic is important because, as it turns out, all evidence for past evolutionary events (such as the divergence of man from primates, for example) is derived from inference precisely because they occurred in the past and were not directly observed. The mechanism of biological evolution, i.e., natural selection, is an ongoing process. However, because it is too slow to be directly observed, evidence for natural selection is also based primarily on inferences derived from unsupported premises. Much evidence for evolution also depends on comparisons, which rely on inferences.

3.1 Induction & Deduction

Induction and deduction are two forms of inference. In both cases, conclusions are drawn from a set of starting conditions, or premises. Deductive inference may produce necessarily true conclusions and thus appears powerful at first, but deduction is actually the weaker of these two forms of inference. The reason deduction can produce necessary conclusions is because it moves from the general to the particular. That is, the conclusion is actually already contained within the major premise. For example, birds are defined as animals with feathers. When we observe that a chicken has feathers and subsequently deduce that chickens are birds, we have classified chickens but not learned anything fundamentally new.

Premise 1: Animals with feathers are birds (by definition).
Premise 2: Chickens are animals with feathers (an observation).
Conclusion: Chickens are birds.

Notice how in the above argument we move from the general (all animals with feathers) to the particular (chickens). Also, in deductive argument a theory is a starting point assumed to be established fact. In the example above, "animals with feathers are birds" is not just a definition, it is a working framework, or theory.

By contrast, induction moves from the particular to the general and the theory is the grand finale of induction. The conclusions, or theories, of induction can be probable (even highly probable), but they cannot be definitively proved. So, while a conclusion from a deductive argument can be necessarily true, deduction cannot expand our total body of knowledge. On the other hand, induction can expand our total body of knowledge, but the conclusions are always tentative.

Darwin's hypothesis is often called a theory. If it's a theory, it's a deductive theory – one assumed to be true and providing the starting framework for interpreting observations. Just as historical science is conflated with empirical science to bolster Darwinism, so are deductive theory and inductive theory blurred to make evolution appear to be the grand finale of numerous pieces of evidence rather than the starting point for interpreting data.

Deductive logical arguments are constructed of premises that lead to conclusions. A premise may be true or false, and an argument may be constructed properly (valid) or improperly (invalid). A valid deductive argument with true premises leads to a necessarily true conclusion. Note, *validity* refers only to the construction of the argument, not the truthfulness of its premises or conclusion. A valid deductive argument may lead to a false conclusion if it contains a false premise. Thus, deduction can lead to necessarily true conclusions or false conclusions depending on the truthfulness of the premises and / or the validity of the argument. A deductive argument that is constructed properly (i.e., is valid) and contains true premises is called *sound*. Many deductive arguments contain at least one premise that is true by definition, as we saw in the chicken example above. Others contain premises that are assumed truths. Obviously, the soundness of the argument depends on the actual truthfulness of the premises.

Inductive arguments are also constructed of premises that lead to conclusions. And, again, the premises may be true or false, and the argument may be constructed properly or improperly. In the case of inductive arguments, a properly constructed argument is said to be strong and an improperly constructed argument is weak. A strong inductive argument with true premises is said to be cogent.

Thus,

A strong inductive argument + true premises = cogent argument, and

A valid deductive argument + true premises = sound argument.

The correctness of the conclusion is not always dependent upon the truthfulness of the premises or the validity of the argument. That is, an invalid argument may still provide a true conclusion by accident. Usually, however, an invalid argument leads to a false conclusion. Fallacies are various forms of invalid arguments.

3.1.1 Hypotheticals

Although arguments must be constructed according to certain rules, logical arguments may be constructed in several ways. One common form is the "If... then" construction, or hypothetical. Both inductive and deductive arguments can be framed as hypotheticals. As stated already, in deduction we start with a definition or a theory assumed to be true. In this example, we use the definition "Animals with feathers are classified as birds" as our starting framework. To determine if an animal fits the classification, we use the hypothetical: "If an animal has feathers, then it is a bird." Upon observing a chicken we note that it is an animal with feathers. We thus conclude that chickens are birds based on this observation. As long as the premises are true (i.e., animals with feathers are birds and chickens are animals with feathers), then the conclusion that chickens are birds is necessarily true.

3.1.2 The Cell Theory: An Example of Induction

Induction starts not with the theory but with an observation. We can use the Cell Theory as an example of how induction is used in science.

Cells were first observed in the mid-1660s shortly after the invention of the microscope. By the early 1800s, Matthias Jakob Schleiden had concluded from his observations that all plants are composed of cells or cell-made parts while his contemporary Theodor Schwann had concluded the same about animal cells. In 1839, Schwann proposed what has since become known as the Cell Theory, which postulated that 1) all living things are composed of one or more cells and 2) cells form the basic functional unit of life. During that time, the origin of cells was a hotly debated topic. In the 1850s Rudolf Virchow proposed the third tenet of the Cell Theory: all cells arise only from pre-existing cells. The work of Louis Pasteur in the 1860s and 70s falsified the hypothesis of spontaneous generation and affirmed that even bacteria are born from pre-existing bacteria. The maxim was extended to Omne vivum ex vivo ("all life from life").

So, we first observed that plants are made of cells and all plant cells are formed by the division of pre-existing plant cells. We noticed a pattern when we observed that all animals are made of cells and all new animal cells are formed by the division of pre-existing animal cells, and even bacteria reproduce by the division of pre-existing bacteria cells. We then proposed a theory to explain these observations: the Cell Theory, which states that all living things are made of cell and cells reproduce by the division of pre-existing living cells. Notice how our inductive argument progressed from the particular (animal cells, plant cells, bacteria cells) to the general (all cells) and began with observations and ended with a theory, which is really a grand proposal.

3.1.3 The Hypothetico-Deductive Method

In Chapter 2, we noted that Isaac Newton described empirical science as an inductive process. According to D. Q. McInerny, author of *Being Logical: A Guide to Good Thinking*: "The whole scientific enterprise is built upon induction." However, in practice scientists use induction and deduction in a rather circular way to explore the world (Figure 3-1). Indeed, inductive argument forms the basis for deductive argument and experimentation. Let us retrace the development of the Cell Theory. We saw how induction was used to formulate the theory: plant cells were observed to come from living plant cells, animal cells were observed to come from living animal cells, bacteria were observed to come from living bacteria. Therefore, it was concluded that all cells come from pre-existing like cells. With that, we can now formulate the following deductive hypothesis: If all cells reproduce by the division of pre-existing living cells (now taken as a given), then yeast cells will reproduce by division of pre-existing living yeast cells. Subsequent observations confirm this deductive hypothesis and corroborate our inductive conclusion (the Cell Theory).

So far, we've concluded that all cells come from pre-existing cells, but do they come *only* from pre-existing cells? We can further refine our theory by hypothesizing that the only way new cells are born is by the division of pre-existing cells. Louis Pasteur devised experiments to test this hypothesis. For example, Pasteur killed all living bacteria cells in a culture flask and kept the flask clean of outside contamination. The result: no bacteria grew inside a sterile flask with ample food supply. If many such experiments fail to disqualify our hypothesis, then it remains provisionally corroborated and our Cell Theory is refined.

The current Cell Theory does in fact state that all cells come only from the division of pre-existing living cells. Although tested by experiment on deductive hypotheses, this theory is the conclusion of an inductive argu-

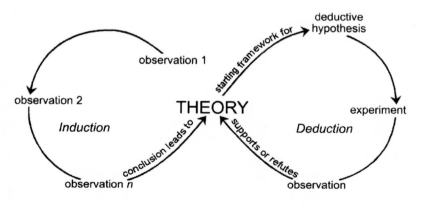

Figure 3-1: The inductive/hypothetico-deductive cycle used in research.

ment and recall that inductive conclusions can only be probable, they cannot be definitively proven. If it were observed that fungal cells or any other cells are born by some other mechanism than cell division, our assumed truth, i.e., our hypothesis, that all cells reproduce by cell division would be falsified, as would our inductive conclusion, the Cell Theory. We may yet find cells that come into existence some other way, but so far no other way has been observed.

Notice that simple deduction can provide necessarily true conclusions because it is based entirely on definitions or assumed truths, induction can only provide tentative conclusions, and deductive hypotheticals are assumed truths or definitions that can be tested by experiment and thereby falsified. The latter is technically called the hypothetico-deductive method and is more generally known as the scientific method. The hypothesis is an assumed truth that is put to the test for verification.

3.1.4 The Syllogism

The if... then hypothetical is one way to frame an argument. The syllogism is another common construction for logical arguments. The Syllogism consists of two declarative premises and a conclusion. Few arguments in books or conversation are framed in syllogism format, but converting those arguments to syllogisms is a useful way to probe the logic of those arguments. Consider the following examples:

Example #1:
Premise 1: All feathered animals are birds (true by definition).
Premise 2: Chickens are feathered animals (true by observation).
Conclusion: Therefore, chickens are birds (necessarily true).

Example #2:
Premise 1: Apples are fruit (true).
Premise 2: Bananas are fruit (true).
Conclusion: Therefore, apples are bananas (false).

Example #3:
Premise 1: Sweet things are made of sugar (true).
Premise 2: Babies are sweet (true).

Conclusion: Therefore, babies are made of sugar (false).

Example #1 demonstrates a logical argument with true premises and a proper construction; it is a sound argument that gives rise to a necessarily true conclusion. Example #2 contains two true premises but is invalid because it is improperly constructed (it has an *undistributed middle[50]*). It leads to a false conclusion. Example #3 has two true premises (premise 2 is actually an opinion, or statement of value, not a fact; for the moment we will accept it as true), but the conclusion is patently false. The argument is invalid because it commits a fallacy called *equivocation*: two different definitions are being employed for the word "sweet."

As I've said already, evidence for biological evolution is based entirely on inference rather than direct observation, much of it based on simple deduction fraught with fallacies. In the example that follows in Section 3.2, evolutionist Neil Shubin uses a common but unsound deductive inference to conclude an evolutionary relationship between humans and bats.

3.2 The Logic of Darwinism

In the 1800s Sir Richard Owen realized that the skeletons of many animals share a basic design theme. For instance, humans, frogs, bats, whales and many other limbed creatures share the following skeletal arrangement with

---

Simple Deduction: All feathered animals are birds (which is true by definition), and chickens are animals with feathers (which is true by observation). Therefore, it is *necessarily true* that chickens are birds.

Induction: Human cells reproduce only by cell division (observed), plant cells reproduce only by cell division (observed), bacterial cells reproduce only by cell division (observed). Therefore, it's *probably* true that all cells reproduce only by cell division.

Deductive Hypothetical: If it's true that all cells reproduce only by cell division (assumed truth), then yeast cells will reproduce by cell division. Experiment and observation will falsify or corroborate the hypothesis.

---

their limbs: one upper bone → two lower bones → a collection of wrist/ankle bones → five digits (the arrow means "connected to"). A comparison of human and bat limbs is shown in Figure 3-2. In his book, *Your Inner Fish*, Neil Shubin concludes (as do other evolutionists) that the skeletal arrangement shared by these organisms is evidence for common ancestry. Shubin writes:

"Shortly after Owen announced this observation in his classic monograph On the Nature of Limbs, Charles Darwin supplied an elegant explanation for it. The reason the wing of a bat and the arm of a human share a common skeletal pattern is because they shared a common ancestor. The same reasoning applies to human arms and bird wings, human legs and frog legs – everything that has limbs."

Unfortunately for Shubin and Darwin, that same reasoning is logically flawed. In a logical-argument form, the reasoning goes like this:

Premise 1: A human limb has 1-bone → 2-bones → many-bones → 5 digits.
Premise 2: A bat limb has 1-bone → 2-bones → many-bones → 5 digits.
Conclusion: Therefore, humans and bats are ancestrally related.

Shubin's argument is invalid for the same reason as our Example #2 in Section 3.1.4 above; it has an undistributed middle. In addition, the conclusion simply does not follow from the premises (*non sequitur*). To illustrate this point more clearly, let us reformulate the argument using a non-biological example.

Premise 1: A car has wheels with tires and brakes.
Premise 2: A plane has wheels with tires and brakes.
Conclusion: Therefore, cars and planes are ancestrally related.

It's easy to see that the conclusion above is false, yet it is the same logic used in the limb example. One could argue that the situation is not analogous because humans and bats reproduce sexually, cars and planes do not. That is true, but the logical fallacy remains. Humans and bats *could* be ancestrally related, but, as our cars and planes demonstrate, that conclusion does not necessarily follow from the premises supplied. In other words, bats and humans could be related, but the structural similarities between them do not constitute evidence for that conclusion. One could just as easily con-clude that all those limbs are similar because they were designed by a com-mon engineer (God). Either way, it's also perfectly logical that these limbs would share a similar structure because they perform similar functions, i.e., the limbs are examples of the Structure-Function Principle. The similarities are not evidence for a common ancestry.

The syllogism is a logical argument format that follows the structure A is B and B is C, therefore A is C. When Neil Shubin's argument is structured as a syllogism, we see that it fails because it commits the fallacy of having an undistributed middle term. However, the argument can also be stated as a *conditional argument*, i.e., a hypothetical, using the If/then format as fol-lows:

Hypothetical: If bats and humans are ancestrally related, then they will share the same skeletal pattern.
Observation: Bats and humans share the same skeletal pattern.
Conclusion: Therefore, bats and humans are ancestrally related.

Framed in this way (actually a mixed hypothetical syllogism), the argu-ment is invalid because it commits the fallacy of *affirming the consequent*. The antecedent of the major premise tells us that a specific condition must be met (bats and humans *must* be related) in order for a specific consequent to follow (share a skeletal pattern). However, the statement does not dic-tate that this is the *only* condition which will necessitate the consequent and, in fact, there are other conceivable reasons why bats and humans share a skeletal pattern, such as the consistent use of the pattern by an intelligent designer. Evolutionists who reject God *a priori* may believe that common descent is the only conceivable way bats and humans could share the same skeletal pattern or genetic code, or any number of other similarities, but their self-imposed restriction only limits their options, not reality. Of course, the creationist version of this argument would be guilty of the same fallacy:

Hypothetical: If bats and humans were created by a frugal designer, then they will share the same skeletal pattern.
Observation: Bats and humans share the same skeletal pattern.
Conclusion: Therefore, bats and humans were created by a frugal designer.

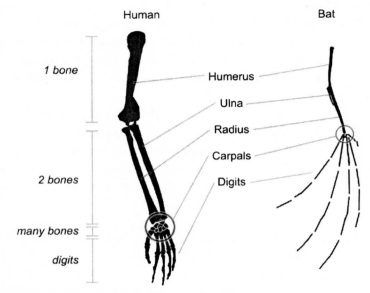

Figure 3-2: Comparison of human and bat limbs.

Thus, either conclusion might be true. A shared skeletal pattern really doesn't shed any light on the question of bat and human origins.

For clarity, here is another example of affirming the consequent with a more obviously false conclusion:

Hypothetical: If Tom Brady plays baseball, then he is an athlete.
Observation: Tom Brady is an athlete.
Conclusion: Therefore, Tom Brady plays baseball.

Playing baseball is not the *only* way to be an athlete and Tom Brady does not play baseball (though he is a pretty good quarterback).

Can we not correct the fallacy by simply switching the phrases in the hypothetical? Let's try.

Hypothetical: If bats and humans share the same skeletal pattern, then bats and humans are ancestrally related.
Observation: Bats and humans share the same skeletal pattern.

Conclusion: Therefore, bats and humans are ancestrally related.

This conclusion affirms the antecedent and the argument is therefore valid in that respect, but still the hypothetical is *non sequitur* – the consequent simply doesn't follow from the antecedent. Again, the major premise tells us that a specific condition must be met (bats and humans *must* share the same skeletal pattern) in order for a specific consequent to follow (bats and humans are related). I hardly think that evolutionists believe organisms *must* share a skeletal pattern in order to be related. Recall that Darwinists believe that *all* organisms are related by a single common ancestor. If a shared skeletal pattern is the test for relatedness, then clearly many organisms are not related. For example, there can be no shared skeletal pattern between earthworms and humans, so by this hypothetical syllogism earthworms and humans cannot be ancestrally related.

To see this more clearly, refer once more to Tom Brady and switch the phrases in the hypothetical (i.e., If Tom Brady is an athlete, then he must play baseball). The consequent simply does not follow from the antecedent. There are other ways to be an athlete than playing baseball.

It's important to recognize the fallacy in this argument because shared characteristics – be they skeletal patterns, DNA sequences, or innumerable other traits – are routinely taken as powerful confirming evidence for biological evolution by both experts and laymen. For example, the above argument made by Shubin is repeated in the college textbook, *Biology, 10th edition*.

3.3 More Faulty Reasoning by Darwinists

Darwinism is based largely on unsound deductive inferences within a worldview established by coherent truth. It departs from empirical science which is an inductive / hypothetico-deductive enterprise and departs from reality grounded in correspondent truth. The inferences are often logically flawed because they are based on assumptions unsupported by real-world observation. The following examples will illustrate these points.

3.3.1 Confusing Conceptual Facts for Empirical Facts

Worldview (a.k.a., paradigm) was defined in Chapter 2. In his book, *Worldviews*, Richard DeWitt excellently clarifies many worldview issues and leads an engaging walk through the history of science. Throughout most of the book he focuses on physics and philosophy, but at the end of the book he turns to biology to discuss Darwin's hypothesis.

As discussed in Chapter 2, DeWitt delineates between *empirical / objective fact* and *philosophical / conceptual fact*. He spends considerable time highlighting where scientists in the past have confused philosophical facts as empirical evidence. With much anticipation I hoped to see him expose the philosophical facts that dominate the Darwinian worldview. Instead, DeWitt falls into the same trap he had just pages ago revealed to have ensnared so many others. He is completely duped by Darwinism. For instance, on page 279, DeWitt, like Neil Shubin, repeats what is called Berra's blunder (discussed in Section 4.1.3): "We can speak of populations... and generations of cars." He then states explicitly: "In short, evolution need not be thought of as applying only to biological populations." First, DeWitt is clearly using a definition of evolution such as "change over time" and not a definition that includes genes, mutations, heredity, natural selection, or any other peculiars of the biological world. Second, he seems unaware that this sort of evolution – change over time – in fact applies *only* to non-biological entities, specifically only to man-made inventions. It is astounding, really, that DeWitt fails to see that "fashion evolution," i.e., the changing forms of cell phones, hair styles, car styles, etc., is not empirical evidence for biological evolution. Cars, cell phones, computers, etc., change over time ("evolve") because of advances in human technology and personal preferences. This has nothing to do with, and certainly cannot be construed as evidence for, the molecules-to-man claims of Darwinists for the biological world. In short, he has confused a philosophical / conceptual fact for an empirical fact. More precisely, he has transposed an observation about phone styles, car styles, etc., onto the biological world. Evidently, change in the biological world is now a fact because we see change in technology and human fashion styles, but the "fact" that biological organisms change over time is a philosophical / conceptual fact, not an observation of the living world. The change DeWitt so easily imagines in the biological realm is a conceptual fact readily accepted by him because it is coherent with his worldview.

DeWitt devotes several pages of his book to describing computer programs designed by Robert Axelrod and other scientists in the 1970s aimed at demonstrating how altruistic and cooperative behavior could have evolved. At the end his narrative, he praises their work as *firm empirical evidence* for Darwinism. He writes:

> *"From the time of Darwin, there have been speculative proposals about how cooperative and altruistic behavior might have been evolutionarily advantageous. But speculation is one thing, and empirical data another. A key aspect of Axelrod's work is that it provides* **firm empirical data** *relevant to questions such as how cooperative behavior can be evolutionarily advantageous."* (Emphasis added.)

Firm empirical data?!

A few chapters earlier DeWitt stated (correctly) that the eclipse of 1919 provided empirical data that confirmed Einstein's theory of relativity. I wonder, though, if DeWitt would consider a computer simulation of gravity bending starlight to be "firm empirical data" confirming Einstein's theory *in lieu* of the actual observation. This is another astounding display of confusing a conceptual fact for an empirical fact by the man who just spent pages defining these terms and giving numerous examples of others who have tripped over them. In 2012, physicists at the Large Hadron Collider finally detected the elusive Higgs boson after years of searching, but I doubt many would have been convinced of its existence by a mere computer simulation, one programed to obey the rules of the theory being tested. DeWitt has committed a fallacy akin to reification; we might call it virtification – confusing virtual data (a computer simulation) – for something concrete or real.

Again relying on computers and their programs, DeWitt claims that

> *"Altruistic behavior will not necessarily be an evolutionarily stable strategy. That is, one can show (this is generally done through computer modeling) that in some contexts, agents acting altruistically in these sorts of ways will not be reproductively successful enough to ensure that the altruistic tendencies remain in the population. In other contexts, however, such altruistic tendencies can be an evolutionarily stable strategy."*

How, exactly, can one show that altruistic behavior is or is not evolutionarily advantageous, and in which contexts? You cannot, empirically. Thus, these sorts of studies are not "generally done" through computer modeling, they are *only* done through computer modeling (or some other modeling). And let us not ignore the all-encompassing result that altruistic behavior will evolve, unless it doesn't (but it will, because it did).

After concluding that Axelrod's computer program is "firm empirical data" for biological evolution, DeWitt describes another study called the Ultimatum Game. This is not a computer simulation but a game played by real people. It is a game that essentially measures how selfish (or conversely, how altruistic) people are. Note that this is a test of how people behave today, in the here-and-now. On its face, this test has nothing to do with evolution. However, DeWitt believes the limited empirical facts from this study describe something more than they actually do. He converts empirical data that supports proposition X into philosophical / conceptual facts that support proposition Y in his worldview. DeWitt notes that the results from this test are similar for volunteers ranging from American college students to nomadic tribes. This is an observed result – an empirical fact. But this empirical fact slips into philosophical fact when he concludes: "Behavior that is this consistent across cultures suggests that the behavior is stemming from more deeply ingrained tendencies. And tendencies that are deeply ingrained in this way are almost certainly a result of our evolutionary past."

Of course, a creationist could just as easily interpret the results of the Ultimatum Game like this: "Behavior that is this consistent across cultures suggests that the behavior is stemming from more deeply ingrained tendencies. And tendencies that are deeply ingrained in this way are almost certainly a result of ~~our evolutionary past~~ *all men being made in the image of God*."

Don't be fooled. Words like "suggests" and "almost certainly" are not a demonstration of politeness or modesty. Rather, they give away the weakness of these arguments.

Does the Ultimatum Game provide an empirical fact or a philosophical fact about humanity? Both. It provides an empirical fact with respect to modern human behavior, but only a philosophical / conceptual fact regarding whatever this means about the origins of modern human behavior.

DeWitt continues to describe additional studies that "investigated the conditions under which these sorts of cooperative and altruistic behaviors are and are not successful." Unfortunately, he does not actually cite the studies or their authors, so I could not review the original sources myself. However, he claims the studies conclude that conditions that favor altruism existed 100,000 – 200,000 years ago, happily at just the time our ancestors branched into our lineage. What were those conditions? Small group size is one, and DeWitt assures us that "early humans were almost certainly members of relatively small group size." How he comes to this conclusion is a mystery. A second condition is limited migration into and out of the group. Again, according to DeWitt, "a likely condition present with early humans." And yet again, a mystery as to how he knows this. A third condition is "where there is likely to be substantial competition with other groups." Not surprisingly, DeWitt finds it easy to imagine that such competition and conflict was likely among early humans. DeWitt concludes, "These results are preliminary. But results such as these nicely illustrate some of the ways issues involved in our ethical behavior can be studied *empirically*." (Emphasis added).

Richard DeWitt literally wrote the book on scientific worldviews and how to distinguish philosophical / conceptual facts from empirical facts. He then promptly made every mistake in the book with respect to origins science. The fact that DeWitt himself fails to see where he blatantly mistakes philosophical facts for empirical facts nicely demonstrates how blinded we all can be by our own worldview.

DeWitt also provides one of the best examples of confusing empirical science with historical science. He writes: "Questions about the origin of the universe, about the way events in the universe unfold, about the development of life – are empirical questions. As they are empirical questions, we should look to the empirical evidence to decide on the most reasonable views about such matters." Indeed, his entire book is one long confusion of empirical and historical sciences. DeWitt spends 26 chapters discussing empirical science (mainly physics) and how our worldview doctrines progressed from age-to-age as our understanding of how the universe operates increased, then he makes a sudden switch to biology and Darwin's hypothesis without ever acknowledging the switch from empirical to historical science and, indeed, explicitly calls the questions of history "empirical questions."

In his book, DeWitt claims – like so many evolutionists do – that "evolutionary theory is supported by overwhelming empirical evidence." But, not trivially, the only evidence he provides is a computer simulation and a social study on contemporary human behavior. Surely if one is writing a book on scientific revolutions and claiming that the current revolution fueled by Darwin's dangerous idea is "supported by overwhelming empirical evidence," then one could present better *empirical* data than that. We are driven to conclude that when someone claims Darwinism is supported by overwhelming evidence what they really mean is that Darwinism fits their worldview so well that they feel an overwhelming sense of its rightness. But, as unwittingly demonstrated by DeWitt himself, the Darwinian worldview is built almost entirely on philosophical / conceptual facts mistaken as empirical facts.

3.3.2 Chromosome Fusion: A Leap-to-Conclusion

Darwinian evolution has never been *observed*. Think about that. By Darwinian evolution I mean speciation or even any "positive" change within a species that doesn't come with a fitness cost. Lacking direct observation, we find that the whole theory relies entirely on simple deductive inference, as all historical sciences must. This weakens the hypothesis of biological evolution but does not condemn it to the dustbin of failed hypotheses. Indeed, the entire scientific enterprise depends upon inference. The difference between Darwinism and empirical science, however, is that inferences made in science must be put to the test and by observation of the results the inference is either supported or rejected. The past events of Darwinism cannot be put to the test and the *mechanism* of Darwinism fails the test. Ultimately, what condemns evolution is the consistent use of false premises and invalid arguments that lead to predictably false conclusions. Those conclusions are nonetheless hailed as truth by Darwinists and then subsequently used as premises for future bad arguments.

The story of human chromosome 2 fusion nicely demonstrates how invalid arguments are used by evolutionists to obtain false (or at best dubious) conclusions which are then presented as hard conclusions and newly established fact.

Due to the obvious similarities between humans and primates, it should not be surprising to find that we share a high degree of DNA sequences and a similar chromosome arrangement. We expect these similarities because of the Structure-Function Principle. However, it is observed that humans have 23 chromosome pairs whereas apes have 24 chromosome pairs. The Structure-Function Principle should have been enough to prompt a search for either a chromosome fusion in humans or a chromosome split in apes once the discrepancy was noted. It was *not* this principle but an anticipated ancestral relationship between apes and humans that prompted the search. In any case, upon looking for it, it was discovered that human chromosome 2 has an extra, inactive centromere and an internal, inactive telomere-telomere fusion (Figure 3-3). These observations strongly suggest that humans, like apes, originally had 24 chromosome pairs and that 2 pair fused. Clearly, this fusion occurred long ago because every human (we think) possesses only 23 chromosome pairs.

When the fusion was found in humans, the simple conclusion that two human chromosomes conjoined long ago in human history is a parsimonious and sufficient explanation, but evolutionists cannot resist inferring an ancestral relationship between humans and apes based on this data. A description of this chromosome fusion on Wikipedia plainly asserts the common sentiment: "Chromosome 2 presents very strong evidence in favor of the common descent of humans and other apes."[51] The Wikipedia statement rightly reflects the conclusion of the researchers who conducted the study. According to researcher J. W. IJdo: "We conclude that the locus cloned in cosmids c8.1 and c29B is the relic of an ancient telomere-telomere fusion

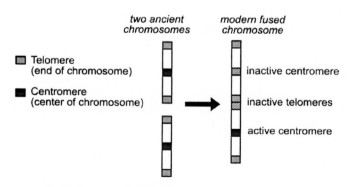

Figure 3-3: Two human chromosomes appear to have fused long ago.

and marks the point at which two ancestral ape chromosomes fused to give rise to human chromosome 2."[52]

The inference looks like this in logical-argument form:

Premise 1: Apes have 24 chromosome pairs.
Premise 2: Humans have 23 chromosome pairs.
Premise 3: Chromosome 2 in humans is empirically shown (i.e., observed) to be a fusion of two chromosomes.
Conclusion: Humans are descended from apes with 24 chromosome pairs, and the "locus cloned... marks the point at which two ancestral ape chromosomes fused to give rise to human chromosome 2."

The logical argument is invalid, however, and the Darwinian conclusion is unjustified. Premise 2 is an empirical fact that can be easily demonstrated by any DNA specialist. Premise 3 is an empirical fact demonstrated by IJdo et al.; two chromosomes in humans fused at some point to form a single chromosome. However, premise 1 is simply irrelevant. The chromosome 2 data is only evidence that two human chromosomes fused in a human ancestor common to all living humans and it is not evidence for common ancestry between humans and apes. Without the insertion of irrelevant premise 1, the sounder conclusion would be thus: "We conclude that the locus cloned in cosmids c8.1 and c29B is the relic of an ancient telomere-telomere fusion and marks the point at which two ancestral ~~ape~~ *human* chromosomes fused to give rise to *modern* human chromosome 2."

Interestingly, the deer mouse also has 24 chromosome pairs, but the authors did not include the deer mouse in premise 1 or conclude an ancestral linkage between men and mice from this chromosome fusion data.

3.3.3 Faulty Extrapolation

As mentioned previously, Stephen J. Gould wrote a lengthy Introduction to a book by Carl Zimmer called *Evolution: The Triumph of an Idea*. In the Introduction, Gould declared that "three broad categories of evidence best express the factuality of evolution. First, direct evidence of human observation."

What!?

Gould quickly clarifies that speciation or other large-scale changes have not been observed, but only "the small-scale changes that our theories anticipate over such geographically brief periods of time." But as usual, large-scale (macro) changes must be inferred from small-scale (micro) changes. The micro-to-macro inference is an extrapolation that looks like this:

1. Small changes can occur to living organisms in short periods of time.
2. Life has been on Earth for a long time.
Therefore, large changes have occurred to living things over long periods of time.

Is the micro-to-macro extrapolation unreasonable? I believe it is. One problem with this argument is its vagueness. What is a "small change" or a "large change" anyway? If we define "large change" as speciation, then – as Gould admits – this has never been observed. The argument also presupposes that numerous, successive "small changes" in living organisms will (or can) eventually result in "large changes" in organisms. Again, this is impossible to defend or refute without strict definitions, but if we assume "large change" is speciation or the emergence of a new genus or family from another (the crux of Darwinism), then we have never seen it happen. In fact, it's not possible to ever see it happen because of the enormous time scales required. Finally, the argument also presupposes that change within organisms is unlimited, but is that really the case?

Let us examine the argument in greater detail. Notice that premise #2 is actually superfluous and can be dropped without consequence so that the argument goes as follows: *Small changes can occur to living organisms in short periods of time, therefore large changes can occur to organisms over long periods of time*. The conclusion does not follow from the premise and the argument commits the fallacy of faulty extrapolation. To make this clear, let's examine a more obvious example (more obvious because it can actually be observed): *A pine tree sapling grows to a height of 10 feet in 10 years, therefore it will grow to 900 feet in 900 years*. Obviously, even though the young tree initially grows at a rate of one foot per year it will not always do so. At some point it reaches a maximum height and then stops growing taller. This is known by direct observation. Thus, the extrapolation is not valid.

For comparison, let's look at another example where the extrapolation is valid. The *Voyager 1* space probe left Earth in 1977. In 2012, the probe officially left our solar system and entered interstellar space. Hurling through space at 38,000 mph, *Voyager 1* traveled 11 billion miles from Earth in 35 years, then turned towards the Earth and snapped a picture (Figure 3-4, the ultimate selfie).[53] In 2047, 70 years after launch, it will be 22 billion miles away. In 2077, 100 years after launch, it will be 33 billion miles away. As long as the spacecraft avoids other objects in space, it will continue to travel away from Earth forever at its current speed so the extrapolation is valid.[54] What these two arguments tell us is that the conclusion from an extrapolation *may* be true but is not *necessarily* true. In the case of the *Voyager 1* space probe, we have every reason to believe the extrapolation is valid for many years to come. In the case of organisms changing dramatically over time and being converted from one species to another, we have little reason for confidence in that extrapolation based on real-world observations both in nature and with artificial selection. Certainly, as mentioned already, the conclusion cannot be verified by direct observation because of the requisite time scales.

Although we do know from observation that premise #1 is true, we may doubt the extrapolation based on the real-world, objective observations that variability in any species appears to be limited, not unlimited. Although

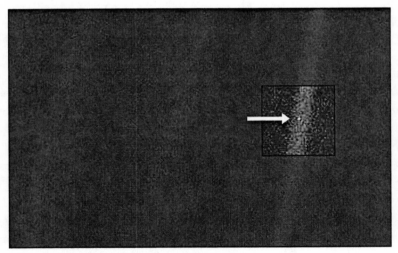

Figure 3-4: View of Earth from *Voyager 1*

any one person can only make direct observations during his own lifetime, we actually have a situation here where direct human observation has been extended through multiple generations in the case of artificial breeding (or artificial selection). It is well known that even after hundreds of years of intense selection breeders have never forced one species to change into another. Indeed, in every case, we observe a maximum amount of variation and then we hit a wall where no more variation can be achieved. This is not a matter of insufficient time. Artificial selection demonstrates − by direct observation − that change within a species, like the growth of our sapling, is limited, not infinite. Ironically, Gould cites artificial selection (in his words: "breeding for improved crop plants and domesticated animals") as evidence for accepting the extrapolation. Indeed, Charles Darwin used artificial selection in his argument for evolution and called it the "best and safest clue" for natural selection. What these men failed to recognize is that artificial selection unambiguously demonstrates the limits of variability. They are asking us to accept an unlimited extrapolation with data that refutes it. Furthermore, artificial breeding is a form of intelligent design since human breeders are manipulating offspring to achieve desired end results. When the human-induced selective pressure is removed, the highly specialized variants revert back to a generic "baramin" (common archetype) within a few generations.[55] These observations hardly seem like arguments for biological evolution.

As evidence for microevolution, Gould included the now debunked peppered moth experiment and the beak size fluctuations of Darwin's finches.[56] Even by the mid-1980s (Gould died in 2002) it was evident that the beak size of Galapagos finches was cyclical, but a more recent study led by two Harvard evolutionists indicates that developmental pathways place "powerful constraints" on beak morphology.[57] Although their findings are consistent with the creationist paradigm and all observations from artificial selection, the authors assure us the findings actually support Darwinism: "[Songbirds] all generate their beaks using the same developmental mechanism, and that puts constraints on the kind of variation they are able to produce," says the lead author in an interview for Harvard Gazette. "Ultimately, it shows how efficiently nature can work, because these birds have been able to squeeze as much as they can from the level of variation they can actually produce."

Collectively, these data reveal that organisms can allow small variations (cyclical in nature or held constant by man) within the confines of well-defined, developmental pathways. As for the peppered moth experiment, it has been thoroughly discredited due to the manifestly unnatural methods employed.[58] These indeed are weak arguments for Gould to be listing as the data that "best express the factuality" of evolution.

In order to even make a micro-to-macro extrapolation, one must be confident that microevolution is itself real. Is it? What is microevolution exactly? Is *any* change in an organism microevolution? Insects have become resistant to pesticides and bacteria have become resistant to antibiotics. Are these examples of microevolution? Under stressful laboratory conditions, bacteria can "evolve" the ability to consume certain new food sources. Is this an example of microevolution? Personally, I do not believe these should be considered examples of microevolution for the same reason that antibody production is not. In these cases, organisms are intelligently modifying proteins to combat antigens, consume new food sources, or defeat a pesticide. Just as mammalian cells can design antibodies to confront novel antigens, so bacteria can sometimes tweak proteins to overcome an antibiotic or consume a new sugar. However, this is a far cry from evolving fundamentally new structures or systems, or morphing into a new species.

"Direct evidence of human observation" was the first of Stephen J. Gould's three broad categories of proofs for biological evolution. The second major category he listed is the fossil record (discussed below and in Section 4.1.3) and the third major category is the "more indirect, but ubiquitous, evidence [that] allows us to draw a clear inference of change from a different historical past by observing the quirks and imperfections, present in all modern organisms, that make no sense except as holdovers from an otherwise altered (that is, evolved) ancestral state." In other words, observations like one bone → two bones → many bones → five digit limbs in various mammals and the "backwards" wiring of the human retina[59] make no sense without evolution (to Gould). By Gould's own admission, however, this third major category depends entirely on inference. But so does his interpretation of the fossil record and his extrapolation of "direct evidence of human observation" based on micro-to-macro evolution. Indeed, all of the evidence for biological evolution rests on inferences rather than direct observations.

3.3.4 Pattern ≠ Ancestry

In his book *Your Inner Fish*, Neil Shubin infers a relationship between humans, polar bears, turtles, and fish from anatomical similarities that become increasingly dissimilar as one moves backward through evolutionary time. He compares organisms with increasingly dissimilar traits to a Russian doll set of groups, sub-groups, sub-sub-groups, etc. In his book, *Why Evolution Is True*, Jerry Coyne agrees with Shubin's conclusion but describes the phenomenon differently. He notes that biologists have for centuries classified organisms and that "different biologists came up with nearly identical groupings... This means," writes Coyne, "that these groupings are not subjective artifacts of a human need to classify, but tell us something real and fundamental about nature. The 'natural' classification is itself strong evidence for evolution."

"Why?" asks Coyne.

> "Because we don't see such a nested arrangement if we're trying to arrange objects that haven't arisen by an evolutionary process of splitting and descent. Take cardboard books of matches, which I used to collect. They don't fall into a natural classification in the same way as living species. You could, for example, sort matchbooks hierarchically beginning with size, and then by country within size, color within country, and so on. Or you could start with the type of product advertised, sorting thereafter by color and then by date. There are many ways to order them, and everyone will do it differently. There is no sorting system that all collectors agree on. This is because rather than evolving, so that each matchbook gives rise to another that is only slightly different, each design was created from scratch by human whim."

How is Coyne wrong in his analogy? First, I'm not sure it's fair to say that "different biologists came up with nearly identical groupings." Few classification schemes were devised prior to the scientific revolution of the Middle Ages. Aristotle is regarded as the first Western thinker to classify organisms and he recognized plants and animals as belonging to two separate kingdoms, which seems so obvious that it can't be missed by anyone. But he further characterized animals primarily on behavior rather than anatomy (i.e., flying animals, walking animals, and swimming animals). The result was obviously quite different than our current scheme, which was devised by

Carolus Linnaeus (1707-1778) and is based on anatomical similarities and differences. Linnaeus' scheme was quickly adopted by other naturalists and so there were no real competing ideas in the West. A classification scheme by a Chinese Buddhist in the first century A.D. mixed anatomy and physiology and thus the Eastern scheme was quite different from the Western approach. To the extent that anatomy alone is used to classify organisms, many features of diverse organisms are so different that they naturally are categorized in a particular way, which brings me to the second error in Coyne's analogy.

The matchboxes that Coyne uses are too closely related to one another to properly make an analogy with biological classification. That is, animals (and plants) are much more diverse than the matchboxes Coyne uses for his analogy. He should be starting with such a diversity of objects as matchboxes, moving boxes, toothpicks, baseball bats, basketballs, baseballs, and soccer balls. Starting with those objects, it is obvious that there are three main groupings: boxes, balls, and sticks. The self-evident similarities and differences in these objects would naturally lead different people to come up with a nearly identical grouping. The subtle differences Coyne describes between matchboxes would be akin to the subtleties that lead naturalists even today to bicker about whether certain similar organisms constitute different species or not. In other words, by using matchboxes only, Coyne is starting classification at the level of species where it is the most difficult to classify.

Neil Shubin and Jerry Coyne, and other evolutionists, infer an ancestral relationship between organisms based on anatomical similarities. Shubin compares organisms of increasingly dissimilar traits to a Russian doll set of groups, sub-groups, sub-sub-groups, etc. Coyne seems to think that a precise classification scheme naturally emerges from this Russian doll set grouping of traits. I agree with Shubin and Coyne on this point; a classification scheme naturally emerges like a Russian doll set if you compare the anatomical traits of many organisms. However, these groupings of traits are simply that – groupings of traits. They do not demonstrate ancestral relationships, just as classification schemes of inanimate objects do not establish ancestry. Indeed, any large collection of items can be grouped as a Russian doll set of increasingly dissimilar traits or depicted as a tree of branching dissimilar traits, as in Figure 3-5. We start with the major classes of objects (boxes, balls, and sticks, in our example) and then subcategorize them based

A. Tree of Things

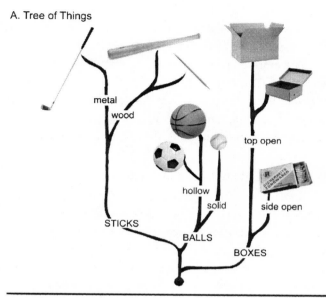

B. Tree of Life

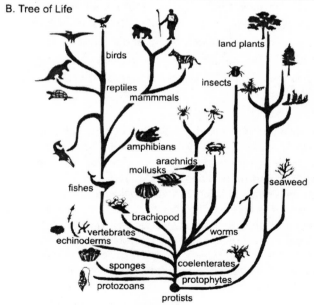

Figure 3-5: Tree of Live vs Tree of Things

on diverging properties, such as solid balls versus hollow balls, wood sticks versus metal sticks, etc. This is a simple example using only a few objects, but with over 8 million species of living things on Earth the Tree of Life can be much more complex. Nevertheless, the Tree of Life and our Tree of Things are nothing more than classification schemes based on shared and unique characteristics. The Tree of Life does not demonstrate descent with modification among living things any more than our Tree of Things does for non-living objects. This is the same faulty reasoning exposed previously regarding bat and human skeletal patterns and ancestry (Section 3.2).

3.3.5 A Straw Man Made of Bait-and-Switch

In his book, *Worldviews: An Introduction to the History and Philosophy of Science*, Richard DeWitt creates a straw man to delegitimize the arguments of creationists. He attempts to deceive us via two episodes of bait-and-switch in one long argument. His argument is ostensibly aimed at describing the difference between *individualistic* and *group* versions of the coherent theory of truth. Recall that the coherent theory of truth states that something is true if it is consistent – or coherent – with other beliefs. I'm not sure it's even valid to distinguish group coherent truths from individual coherent truths since groups are made of individuals and a *group* cannot technically hold a belief, only its individuals can.[60] Nevertheless, DeWitt claims a distinction. You have to read his full argument to grasp the fallacies, so here it is.

> "The different versions of coherence theories differ primarily with respect to whose beliefs are being counted... Are we concerned only with an individual's beliefs, so that, to be true for a particular individual, "The Earth moves about the sun" must merely cohere with that individual's other beliefs? Or are we talking about the beliefs of a group, so that to be true, "The Earth moves about the sun" must cohere with the collective beliefs of that group? And if we are speaking of the beliefs of a group, then who counts as a member of that group? Is it all those who live in a certain geographic region? Is it those who share a particular worldview? Is it the community of scientists or other experts?
>
> "Depending on how such questions are answered, one arrives at various more specific versions of coherence theories. For example, if the beliefs are the beliefs of the individual in question, then we

have what might be called an *individualistic coherence theory. On such a theory, a belief is true for Sara if it fits in with Sara's other beliefs; a belief is true for Fred if it fits in with Fred's other beliefs; and so on. It should be clear that, on an individualistic coherence theory, truth is relative to the individual in question. That is, what is true for Sara may not be true for Fred.*

"*If we opt instead to make the collection of beliefs those of a particular group, we arrive at quite different versions of coherence theories. These might be called group versions of coherence theories. Just for the sake of illustration, suppose we hold that, say, a belief having to do with science is true if it fits in with the collective beliefs of the group of western scientists. For convenience, let us call such a view a science-based version of a coherence theory.*

"*Note that, although the individualistic version and the science-based version are both types of coherence theories of truth, they are quite different theories. To see this, consider an acquaintance of mine, whose name is Steve. Steve quite sincerely and with deep conviction believes that the moon is further from the Earth than the sun is, that the moon is inhabited, and that the moon is a place of frequent parties and other sorts of revelry.*

"*Steve's jigsaw puzzle of beliefs, although quite different from my jigsaw puzzle and probably quite different from yours, forms a system of beliefs that tie together perfectly well. In particular, Steve's belief that the moon is inhabited by intelligent beings coheres with the rest of his beliefs. Thus, on the individualistic version of the coherence theory, Steve's beliefs about the moon are true. Importantly, Steve's beliefs are just as true for him as your beliefs about the moon are for you and mine are for me.*

"*On the other hand, according to a science-based version of the coherence theory, Steve's beliefs about the moon are false, since those beliefs do not cohere with the overall set of beliefs of western scientists. In short, the individualistic version and the science-based version are two different theories of truth, although both of them are types of coherence theories.*"

Okay, that's his argument. Now, let's unpack it and expose the two episodes of bait-and-switch. First, he claims to be comparing two versions of the coherent theory of truth: individualistic versus group. However, early in the argument he switches the name "group version" to "science-based version." This slight-of-hand is aimed at giving this group legitimacy. Second, his science-based version is not actually based on the coherent theory of truth but on the correspondent theory of truth. The *reason* the group of scientists hold their described views of the moon is because those views align with actual observations of the real moon. We've measured the moon's distance from Earth, for example, and we've even visited the moon and confirmed it is uninhabited. To keep the argument genuine, DeWitt would have consistently used the terms *individualistic version* and *group version* of coherent truth and he would have used – for both versions – examples that do not correspond to reality. For instance, Steve could personally believe that the moon is inhabited by little green men while the group believes that the moon is inhabited by little yellow men. These consistencies would have actually kept the spotlight on the differences (which are slight at best) between individual versus group versions of coherent truth. As it is, the whole argument appears to be a straw man erected to set Steve up for mockery, which DeWitt delivers in full force:

> "Steve's beliefs stem largely from a strict literal interpretation of certain religious scriptures. Whether his beliefs are any more or less reasonable than those that stem from a literal interpretation of other religious scriptures is a topic beyond the scope of this chapter. But it is worth mentioning that literal interpretations of religious scriptures often lead to unusual collections of beliefs."

DeWitt chooses a set of beliefs for Steve, and reasons for those beliefs, in a way that is clearly designed to deride Steve (i.e., Christians), while choosing a logical set of beliefs based on actual observations (i.e., correspondent truths) for his group, which he respectfully labeled the "science-based" group. Ironically, DeWitt appears oblivious to the fact that he and other Darwinists hold "a belief having to do with science [that] is true [solely because] it fits in with the collective beliefs of the group of western scientists." Like Steve, Darwinists believe in evolution because it is coherent with their "jigsaw collection of beliefs," not because it corresponds with reality.

Finally, DeWitt is not even talking about "quite different versions of coherence theories" of truth. He is actually comparing two theories about the moon, one held by one group – represented by Steve – and another one held by a different group of individuals called scientists. We must accept, because DeWitt assures us, that those two theories are coherent with other beliefs held by the two parties.

To see how derogatory and hollow this argument really is, let's flip it around:

> *Steve is a creationist, but he is not alone in his views. He is a member of a group called the Church – an organization that has existed for 20 centuries and has millions of members on every continent of the globe. The Church believes there is a God who created Steve and everything else. Now consider Steve's teacher, Professor Dimwiddle, who quite sincerely and with deep conviction believes his great, great grandpa is a monkey. He believes this because it coheres with the rest of his beliefs. On the individualistic version of the coherence theory, Prof. Dimwiddle's beliefs about his ancestors are true, but according to the group-based Church version of truth, Prof. Dimwiddle's beliefs are false.*
>
> *Whether Prof. Dimwiddle's views stem from a revulsion of aged and noble institutions or is simply a desire to fit in with a few thousand colleagues in the group-think Safes Spaces known as American universities is unclear and beyond the scope of this chapter, but it is worth mentioning that being locked away for years in an ivory tower often leads to unusual collections of beliefs.*

3.3.6 The Appeal to Good / Bad Design

Beginning with William Paley and his critics, evolutionists have repeatedly charged creationists with being foolish when they appeal to design inferences in nature. Yet evolutionists employ the same kind of logic in their arguments against intelligent design. Let's compare an argument from Paley with one from evolutionist Neil Shubin.

William Paley once challenged his readers to deny design in the vertebrate eye. He wrote:

> "We find that the eye of a fish, in that part of it called the crystalline lens, is much rounder that the eye of terrestrial animals. What plainer manifestation of design can there be?"

In *Your Inner Fish*, Neil Shubin writes:

> "Looking now at the hind limb we find a key feature that gives us the capacity to walk, one we share with other mammals. Unlike

*fish and amphibians, our knees and elbows face in opposite direc-
tions. This feature is critical: think of trying to walk with your kneecap
facing backward."*

When Shubin asks us to "think of trying to walk with your kneecap facing backward," he is appealing to our sense of design logic, just as Paley did.
Although Shubin, Richard Dawkins, and other Darwinists routinely get away
with it, William Paley and other creationists have been skewered for appealing to design logic.

Ironically, it's not hard to imagine walking with backward knees. George
Lucas imagined it when he created the AT-ST Scout Walker for Star Wars®
(Figure 3-6).[61] Neither is it difficult to imagine that a round fish lens could
evolve over time into a flatter terrestrial lens. The point is, the arguments of
Paley and Shubin are both weak as they rely primarily on imagination rather
than experiment. Indeed, these good design / bad design arguments don't
even depend on an intimate or accurate knowledge of the parts and their
functions. With respect to the focusing mechanism of the eye, Paley asked,
"Can anything be more decisive of contrivance (i.e., purposeful design) than
this?" Unfortunately, he had a complete misunderstanding of the eye's focusing mechanism, believing that the cornea changed shape and the lens
moved back-and-forth to focus light on the retina, neither of which happen.
Nonetheless, as our knowledge of biological systems continues to increase,
the design arguments have been refined in recent years. Most notably, the
introduction of *irreducible complexity* (see Section 4.2.1) from the Intelligent
Design community has moved the argument from imagination and opinion
(good vs bad) to function which relies on the interplay of multiple parts.
Their conclusions support Paley's view.

Shubin devotes an entire section of his book to this line of reasoning
called "Why History Makes Us Sick." Just as nothing made sense to Paley
except in the light of Creation, everything from "hemorrhoids to cancer" is
explained by evolution to Shubin. Evolution and creation are very similar in
this respect – they both explain everything, which is why neither explains
anything scientifically. This is also why neither of them is falsifiable. For
these reasons (and more) they are not science but worldviews, or more precisely, the creation myths of competing worldviews. And they are two sides
of the same coin, or two views of the same photograph, if you prefer; one a
positive and the other a negative. Within each worldview everything makes

sense, but since they are mutually exclusive only one of them can be correct, i.e., correspond to reality.

This particular argument, which we might call an *appeal to good / bad design*, is made surprisingly often by both creationists and evolutionists. We have already seen examples from Paley and Shubin. Richard Dawkins has cited the recurrent laryngeal nerve as an example of bad design. Michael Shermer, Stephen Jay Gould and evolutionists around the world have claimed the retina of the human eye is "wired backwards" and is clear evidence of poor design (or lack of design). To them, the "imperfection" of the eye attests to the twisted and torturous path evolution has taken to advance us from a primitive eye spot to the complex mammalian retina of today. A friend of mine said her college professor claimed no intelligent designer would use the same opening for both respiratory and digestive functions, since this creates an obvious choking hazard; the epiglottis sometimes fails to prevent food from entering the trachea and people choke to death. (This

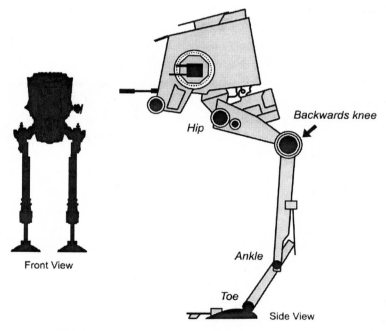

Figure 3-6: The AT-ST Walker featured in Star Wars.

argument was also presented by Neil Shubin in *Your Inner Fish*). Regardless of the particular example you choose, all of these arguments are merely opinion or conjecture. They are not facts. They are value judgments.

Obviously, creationists don't share the same opinions, or value judgments, as evolutionists with respect to body design. The human eye, for example, provides for exceptionally good vision in full color and in real time. The laryngeal nerve successfully communicates nerve impulses to and from the larynx. The larynx works almost flawlessly to produce sound and separate solids and liquids from gases. In other words, these body structures achieve their purposes, and it's hard to argue with success! In addition, there is usually more than one way to achieve a certain goal and it is all too easy as an observer to second-guess the choices of a designer. To conclude that God is a poor designer — or that He does not exist — merely because you have a low opinion of some features of living things is the height of arrogance, in my opinion. In all likelihood, we simply don't have all the necessary information to see the reasons behind the design logic. In the eye, for instance, we do know that photoreceptor cells require enormous amounts of energy and the retina is "wired backwards" to keep those cells near blood vessels, which would be problematically distant or obstruct light if they were wired "correctly." At any rate, declaring something to be poorly designed is nothing more than opinion when that something successfully performs its function.

Evolutionists are clearly schizophrenic when it comes to design. The mammalian retina, the larynx, and the laryngeal nerve illustrate are evidence of evolution to Darwinists because they are so poorly designed. On the other hand, Darwinists claim good design is also evidence for evolution, as we saw with Neil Shubin's praise of the forward-facing kneecap. This is especially odd since Paley and countless other creationists continue to be scorned for appealing to good design as an argument for a Creator. Yet perfection is offered as proof of evolution when speaking of butterflies, frogfish, or other organisms that so impeccably mimic their environment that predators cannot spot them.[62] Below is another example of good design used as an argument for biological evolution, taken from Neil Shubin's *Your Inner Fish*.

"We humans, like many other mammals, can rotate our thumb relative to our elbow. This simple function is very important for the

use of our hands in everyday life. Imagine trying to eat, write, or throw a ball without being able to rotate your hand relative to your elbow. We can do this because one forearm bone, the radius, rotates along a pivot point at the elbow joint. The structure of the joint at the elbow is wonderfully designed for this function."

Besides being an appeal to good design, I would be remiss if I did not point out the anatomical errors presented by Shubin. Shubin describes the radio-humeral joint as a ball-and-socket joint. So as to not mislead the reader on this, I will continue the above quote to get his complete description of the elbow joint:

"The structure of the joint at the elbow is wonderfully designed for this function. At the end of our upper-arm bone, the humerus, lies a ball. The tip of the radius, which attaches here, forms a beautiful little socket that fits on the ball. This ball-and-socket joint allows rotation of our hand, called pronation and supination."

First, Shubin's description of the elbow joint is simply incorrect. The elbow possesses two joints; one is a pivot and the other is a hinge; neither are ball-and-socket. The joint between the humerus and ulna is a classic hinge joint and allows you to flex and extend your forearm in one plane only. The radius possesses a unique cylindrical head that rotates within a ligamentous sheath attached to the proximal end of the ulna.[63] This pivot joint allows supination and pronation of the forearm (Figure 3-7). There is no ball at the

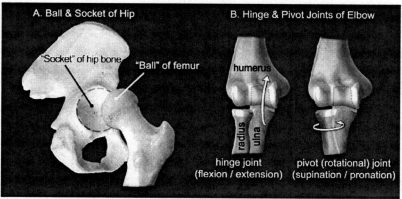

Figure 3-7: Comparison of the elbow joint to a ball-and-socket joint.

distal end of the humerus and no "beautiful little socket" on the radius. There simply is no ball-and-socket joint in the forearm that executes rotation of the hand (supination / pronation). The nearest ball-and-socket joint is the shoulder. In fact, the upper-arm bone (humerus) does not functionally articulate with the radius at all; it articulates with the ulna.

I don't like to harp on this point, but Shubin's description of the elbow is seriously flawed. It would be only a minor gaffe except that it's coming from an expert in a book about understanding human evolution using comparative anatomy. What can I conclude, then, from this error? Either Shubin does not fully understand limb anatomy (not likely), or he has over-simplified the situation for the sake of his lay audience to the point of gross factual error. Either way, it makes it difficult to trust him on matters where I am less knowledgeable when I know he is so plainly in error on matters where I am well-informed.

Shubin's faulty description of the elbow aside, the point is that Darwinists cite examples of perfection in nature to support evolution and they cite examples of imperfection in nature to support evolution. So which is it? It can only be both because the facts in favor of evolution are philosophical / conceptual facts rooted in coherent truth. Darwinism cannot be falsified.

3.3.6.1 Are We Really Designed Poorly?

A friend of mine said her college professor claimed no intelligent designer would use the same opening for both respiratory and digestive functions since that creates an obvious choking hazard. This is an opinion, of course, not a statement of fact.

Science requires numbers, even in biology. Without numbers you have only story-telling. The various appeals to good or bad design are often just conjecture, but I decided to make a calculation of the failure rate of the epiglottis to better determine whether the larynx is poorly designed or not.

I just finished a lunch which consisted of a sandwich, chips, and a glass of milk. I counted the number of times I swallowed during my meal and recorded 76 swallows. Three meals per day, plus another 100 swallows for snacks and roughly 200 swallows for drinking to stay hydrated equals roughly 500 swallows per day or 175,000 swallows per year. The population of the United States is 330 million people, which means that approximately 5.8×10^{13} (i.e., 175,000 x 330 million) swallows are accomplished each year.

A Google search revealed that about 3,000 people choke to death each year in America. The average age in America is 35 years old; assuming the same average age among those who die by choking, then approximately $2x10^{15}$ swallows ($5.8x10^{13}$ x 35) are successfully accomplished per 3,000 choking deaths. Thus, the failure rate of the epiglottis is 3,000 in $2x10^{15}$ swallows, or 1 in 675 billion swallows, or 0.00000000015%. I think we are driven to conclude that the larynx is designed superbly despite the opinion of some evolutionists.

3.3.7 The Designer's Designer

When evolutionists point out "bad design" they are actually attempting to demonstrate a lack of design. However, denying design while staring it in the face is difficult, even for hardcore evolutionists. Francis Crick, the co-discoverer of the structure of DNA, once carped: "Biologists must constantly keep in mind that what they see was not designed, but rather evolved." I'm not sure why this would be necessary if evolution were so obvious and design so preposterous.

Darwinists have, of course, an answer as to why Paley and other creationists (and apparently evolutionists) see design in nature. According to Michael Shermer in *Why Darwin Matters: The Case Against Intelligent Design*, there is an evolutionary advantage to finding patterns in nature. In a rather amazing display of circular reasoning Shermer states:

> *"There is a survival payoff for finding order instead of chaos in the world... which enabled our ancestors to survive and reproduce. We are the descendants of the most successful pattern-seeking members of our species. In other words, we were designed by evolution to perceive design. How recursive!"*

How recursive, indeed.

Shermer, who has somehow seen through Nature's beguiling hoax, believes it is natural to perceive design in nature and to attribute that design to a God. However, he finds a

> *"deep-seated flaw in this argument that undermines the entire endeavor. If the world is complex and looks intricately designed, and therefore the best inference is that there must be a designer, should*

we not then infer that an intelligent designer must itself have been designed? That is, if the earmarks of design imply that there is an intelligent designer, then the existence of an intelligent designer denotes that it must have a designer – a super intelligent designer."

He then claims the super intelligent designer must also have a designer, *ad infinitum.*

Shermer's conclusion is erroneous on at least two counts. First, by definition, God is the Uncaused Cause, the Prime Mover, the Beginner who sets all other causes into motion. Second, the existence of a designer does not necessitate the existence of a designer's designer and if it did, then Shermer's logic would actually present a case *for* a Creator God since we know, for instance, that automobiles are designed by humans. According to Shermer, this fact demonstrates that the automobile designers (i.e., human engineers) must themselves have an intelligent designer (God). Although this is a sound conclusion from Shermer's logic, it is not a sound argument for creationism because his logic is flawed; the existence of a designer does not logically demand the existence of a designer's designer *ad infinitum.*

3.3.8 Explaining Everything

Being a creation myth, Darwinism is not science; it is story-telling. It is a story that encapsulates the worldview and deepest values of those who believe. Darwinism explains everything, and thus it explains nothing. The proof of this is found in the fact that Darwinism cannot be falsified. We've already examined how both perfection and imperfection in nature have been cited as evidence for evolution. Can you imagine any scenario in which Darwinism can be falsified? I cannot. Before I am accused of being unimaginative, let us examines more ways evolution is protected from falsification.

3.3.8.1 Divergent, Convergent, and Living Fossils

According to Darwinists, organisms that once shared a common ancestor can evolve along separate lineages to become very different over time. Humans and chimps supposedly fall into this category, and it is called *divergent evolution.* An article published on the National Museum of Health & Medicine website asked, "Why are human feet different from monkey feet?" They answered:

"Even though the modern human is a primate, and thus a member of the primate family, humans look very different from their monkey cousins. ... Human feet are different from monkey feet because of what we call divergent evolution. Divergent evolution is what happens when a closed population splits off and becomes a new species. The two new species even though closely related start to develop new traits to better help them fit into their environments."[64]

On the other hand, extremely diverse and unrelated organisms, such as bats and birds, may evolve to become strikingly similar, a process called *convergent evolution*. The Public Broadcasting Service (PBS) once marveled over the convergence of two fish species:

"In the frigid waters of the ocean surrounding Antarctica, fish have a special trait which allows them to survive the big chill... It's another of those ingenious evolutionary solutions that seem almost too clever to be true. But consider this: Nature did it not once, but at least twice. Fish at the other end of Earth, in the Arctic, also have antifreeze proteins. But those two populations of fish split long before they developed the antifreeze genes and proteins.

"This is a dramatic example of convergent evolution, when organisms that aren't closely related evolve similar traits as they both adapt to similar environments. There are a finite number of effective solutions to some challenges, and some of them emerge independently again and again. ... Convergent evolution is responsible for the wings of the bat, the bird, and the pterodactyl."[65]

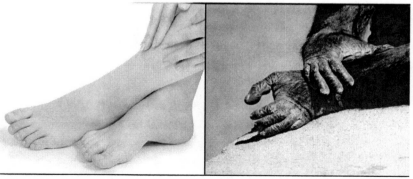

Figure 3-8: Comparison of human feet to ape feet.

Finally, organisms may exist for nearly half-a-billion years without changing at all.[66] The *coelacanth* provides an example of such an organism and these are called *living fossils*. In 2008, a website called www.Dino-Fish.com described the *coelacanth* this way:

> *"Unique in the animal kingdom, with a saga steeped in science and popular imagination, the fabulous Coelacanth ("see-la-kanth"), that 400 million year old "living fossil" fish, swims on – a biological Time Machine. Pre-dating the dinosaurs by millions of years and once thought to have gone extinct with them, 65 million years ago, the Coelacanth with its "missing link" "proto legs" was "discovered" alive and well in 1938."*

Thus, Nature causes organisms to change, except when she doesn't. And when she does, she causes them to become different, except when she causes them to become similar. In other words, the theory of evolution can explain any observation and cannot be falsified by any existing evidence. This is not science; this is story-telling. In addition, Darwinists cannot predict how organisms might change in the future and even if bold predictions were made, they could not be verified by observation. The *coelacanth* was long regarded as a "missing link" fish with proto legs that allegedly ventured onto land millions of years ago, until it was found still swimming in the ocean. Indeed, *coelacanth* provides an excellent example of the dangers associated with inference and the power of direct observation: those chunky fins believed from fossils to be strong enough to support a fish on land are not that strong at all. The fish can swim, but it can't walk (Figure 3-9).

The *coelacanth* is just one of many missing links that turned out not to be a link at all. When a living *coelacanth* was pulled from the water in 1938, it was reclassified as a living fossil. Let us examine another failed missing link courtesy of Tim Berra and Charles Darwin himself.

3.3.8.2 *Archaeopteryx and the Transitional Fossil Problem*

In his book *Evolution and the Myth of Creationism*, Tim Berra agrees with Karl Popper that a theory that cannot be falsified is not a scientific theory. I agree, as well. But it seems that Darwinism is as guilty as creationism in the court of unfalsifiability and with good reason: neither are science; both are

A. *Coelacanth* as presented by Darwinists for many years

B. A living *coelacanth*

Smithsonian National Museum of Natural History (vertebrates.si.edu)

Figure 3-9: Actual *coelacanth* vs the Darwinists' illustration.

creation myths. Nevertheless, as two competing hypotheses about the history of the world, they can be examined scientifically as long as we distinguish empirical science from historical science and remain aware of the inherent weakness of inference compared to experiment and observation. Since we are comparing two versions of history, the best we can do is try to determine which version is the most robust.

Charles Darwin predicted that the fossil record would provide a long and continuous line of intermediates. Indeed, Chuck surmised that the Earth must be littered with countless examples of transitional fossils. However, despite enormous effort, this prediction has most definitely not been vindicated in the 150 years since Darwin made it. Even Darwin could see the problem when he stated:

> *"The number of intermediate varieties which have formerly existed on earth must be truly enormous. Why then is not every geological formation and every stratum full of such intermediate links? Geology assuredly does not reveal any such finely graduated organic chain; and this, perhaps, is the most obvious and gravest objection which can be urged against my theory."*

However, Berra attempts to deflect this objection in his aforementioned book with the following:

> *"It is not reasonable to expect every single species that ever lived, or even very many of them, to show up in the fossil record. There will always be gaps owing to the nature of fossilization and the chanciness of discovery... Thus, transitional forms between species **should be rare** in the fossil record." (Emphasis in original).*

Lest we begin to get suspicious, Berra reassures us that *"Such a statement is not made to protect evolution from falsification but to warn how rare such fossils are likely to be. That even one transitional fossil is found is sufficient demonstration of evolution and a resounding falsification of creationism."* (Emphasis in original).

To claim that n=1 is sufficient to support such a grand theory as Darwinism seems, well, insufficient, but there are other serious flaws with such a claim. For one, alleged transitional forms come and go like the wind. We've already noted that the missing link *coelacanth* is alive and well in the oceans. In his book, Berra spent several pages detailing the reptile-bird *Archaeopteryx* prior to writing the words quoted above. He considered it the "one transitional fossil" sufficient to falsify creationism. The only problem is that while Berra was writing his book a battle was raging over *Archaeopteryx*, one which ultimately ended with the dinosaur-bird being knocked from its perch. Only two of the eleven fossils of *Archaeopteryx* possess feathers, both discovered in the late 1800s by a father and son in a region in Germany.

In 1975, researchers were claiming that had those two specimens not possessed feathers, then the others "would unquestionably have been labeled as coelurosaurian dinosaurs."[67] In 1984, one evolutionary scientist had determined that "*Archaeopteryx* is not an ancient bird, nor is it an 'ideal intermediate' between reptiles and birds."[68] And by 2011, it was definitively decided by the Darwinist community that *Archaeopteryx* was a dinosaur, not a bird and not a transition. In one of the premier science journals, *Nature*, it was written:

> "It's been a good run for Archaeopteryx. For the past 150 years, the famous feathered fossil species from Bavaria and Germany has been a symbol of evolution, a textbook example of a transitional fossil. On page 465 of this issue, however, Xu and colleagues [present evidence] knocking Archaeopteryx off its celebrated perch and moving it and its kin into the great unwashed ranks of 'non avian' dinosaurs."[69]

In other words, *Archaeopteryx* is one big mistake (if not a fraud). But while *Archaeopteryx* was quietly dethroned among scientists, the general population heard little of it. What you've been told in books sold to the general public is that "not to perceive its transitional nature is to be willfully blind to the obvious."[70] This is the *modus operandi* of Darwinists: A transitional form is discovered and the headlines make huge waves in the media, then years later (or less) the fossil is determined to in fact *not* be a transitional form, but the correction is buried somewhere on page 10 if it even gets a mention at all. It happened to the *coelacanth*. It happened to *Archaeopteryx*.

Even more recently, "One of our closest long-lost relatives may never have existed," writes Colin Barras in New Scientist.[71] "The fossils of *Australopithecus sediba*, which promised to rewrite the story of human evolution, may actually be the remains of two species jumbled together." *Australopithecus sebida* graced the covers of both *Science* and *Scientific American* when it was believed to be a missing link, but not when the corrections were announced in 2014.

By the way, *Archaeopteryx* is still the textbook example of a transitional fossil. For example, on page 424 of the college textbook *Biology, 10th edition*, published in 2014, we read:

"Given the low likelihood of fossil preservation and recovery, it is not surprising that there are gaps in the fossil record. Nonetheless, intermediate forms are often available to illustrate how the major transitions in life occurred.

"Undoubtedly the most famous of these is the oldest known bird, Archaeopteryx (meaning "ancient feather") which lived around 165 million years ago (MYA). This specimen is clearly intermediate between birds and dinosaurs. Its feathers, similar in many respects to those of birds today, clearly reveal that it is a bird. Nonetheless, in many other respects – for example, possession of teeth, a bony tail, and other anatomical characteristics – it is indistinguishable from some carnivorous dinosaurs. Indeed, it is so similar to these dinosaurs that several specimens lacking preserved feathers were misidentified as dinosaurs and lay in the wrong natural history cabinets for decades before the mistake was discovered!"[72]

Notably, the biology textbook quoted above fails to mention the controversial history of *Archaeopteryx* or its new classification, or that X-ray and chemical analyses performed in the 1980s definitively demonstrated that the winged *Archaeopteryx* fossils were forgeries. However, the textbook authors are right when they go on to state: *"Archaeopteryx reveals a pattern commonly seen in intermediate fossils."* Indeed, a pattern of wishful thinking and fraud.

In addition, and perhaps more importantly for our current discussion on logic and reason, a transitional fossil can never be proved as such anyway. That is, it can never be demonstrated to actually be related to organisms before it and after it in a supposed lineage. Most fossils are composed entirely of mineral or are often nothing more than an impression left in rock. Consequently, evolutionist are left making inferences based on the structures of the organisms. Finding a fossil of an organism that shares trait X with one organism and trait Y with another does not demonstrate an ancestral relationship (see Section 3.3.4). All it really demonstrates is that humans are adept at finding patterns. Digging up a spork in the vicinity of a spoon and fork does not demonstrate ancestry between these utensils (Figure 3-10). By the way, transitional fossils are rarely found *in vicinity* of each other; the fork may be found in Asia, the spoon in Africa, and the spork in North America and still Darwinists will claim ancestral relationships.

Notably, just twenty pages before his description of *Archaeopteryx*, Tim Berra proclaimed that the fossil record "presents some of the most dramatic evidence for evolution."

3.3.8.3 Deep Time: Pure Science Fiction

Reading the section "Deep Time" in *Biology, 10th edition* is truly an astonishing experience. It is pure science fiction packaged as empirical fact in a college-level science textbook. At least the authors acknowledge several times in the 8-page chapter that historical science exists (not in those words, of course) and that everything they say is inferred (again, they don't say it so bluntly). For instance:

> *"Although is it impossible to be certain what early Earth was like, geological evidence is consistent with a meteor hitting the Earth almost 4.6 billion years ago with such force that that debris from the impact formed the Moon."*

The geological evidence is not presented and one wonders if the mere existence of the Moon is their evidence. And why 4.6 billion years ago? Be-

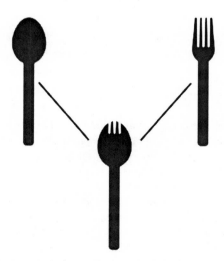

Figure 3-10: Spork ancestor to spoon and fork.

cause that is sufficiently long ago to sound about right? After several paragraphs of this completely fictional creation story, the authors proclaim triumphantly: "At some point, life emerged."

In the next three pages we read that organic molecules may have originated from space, or they may have originated on Earth. Long chains of RNA nucleotides "could have concentrated on clay surfaces and that bonds would have [*would have?*] formed, linking the concentrated nucleotides." The sheer volume of speculation is stunning. After three more pages of more science fiction the authors concede: "We don't know exactly how cells formed because we can't recreate that process, but at some point simple cellular life evolved." This is sheer speculation concluded from pages of imaginative story-telling.

The authors do attempt to show some evidence for early life: a microscopic speck of dust that some have "interpreted as being biological in origin. Although this interpretation has been controversial."

Anything is possible, it seems, except *In the beginning, God...*

3.4 No Reason for Reason

The above examples (Sections 3.3.1 through 3.3.8) are but eight instances of faulty reasoning used by evolutionists. There are many more examples that could be given, but from these it seems already apparent that the pillars of evolution are built on threadbare inferences rather than solid observations. Even more remarkable, the logic of inference itself may be illegitimate in the Darwinian worldview. Regarding the use of inference in the "scientific creation story" (as physicists Brian Cox calls it), C.S. Lewis remarked:

> "Deepening distrust and final abandonment of [the scientific creation story] long preceded my conversion to Christianity. Long before I believed Theology to be true I had already decided that the popular scientific picture at any rate was false. One absolutely central inconsistency ruins it. The whole picture professes to depend on inference from observed facts. Unless inference is valid, the whole picture disappears. Unless we can be sure that reality in the remotest nebula or the remotest part obeys the thought laws of the human scientist here and now in his laboratory – in other words, unless Reason is an absolute – all is in ruins. Yet those who ask me to believe this world picture also ask me to believe that Reason is simply the

unforeseen and unintended by-product of mindless matter at one stage of its endless and aimless becoming. Here is flat contradiction. They ask me at the same moment to accept a conclusion and to discredit the only testimony on which that conclusion can be based. The difficulty is to me a fatal one; and the fact that when you put it to many scientists, far from having an answer, they seem not to even understand what the difficulty is, assures me that I have not found a mare's nest but detected a radical disease in their whole mode of thought from the very beginning."[73]

Lewis' astute observation not only summarizes the problem with inference in the Darwinian worldview, he strikes upon the equally astounding observation that Darwinists are seemingly incapable of seeing the problem. This is what I was referring to in Section 2.5 when I said that Darwinists seem almost universally unable to grasp the reality that Darwinism is a paradigm and evolution theory the creation myth of that paradigm rather than science. But without a reason for reason, there's no reason to believe Darwinism is reasonable.

Although the vast majority of evolutionists seem blind to the mythical and worldview aspects of Darwinism, this reality has been admitted by a few evolutionists who grasp the fact. Among them is Professor D.M.S. Watson who famously declared: "Evolution itself is accepted by zoologists not because it has been observed to occur or... can be proved by logically coherent evidence to be true, but because the only alternative, special creation, is clearly incredible."[74] And by clear implication, unacceptable.

Anything is possible, except *In the beginning, God...*

3.5. The Problem with Comparisons

Virtually all of the evidence for past evolution of life on Earth is comparative, from whole organisms and fossils to molecules. However, it is impossible to establish ancestral relationships by simply comparing two objects, whether those objects are anatomical structures (living or fossilized), proteins, or DNA sequences.[75] All conclusions made from these comparisons are unprovable, yet these constitute *all* of the evidence for past biological evolution. They are conceptual facts that establish a coherent truth, but not necessarily a correspondent truth grounded in reality. The entire Tree of Life is built from simple deductive inferences, not hypothetico-deductive inferences.

Hence, the inferences used to conclude evolution cannot be empirically tested.

The *mechanism* of evolution, Darwin's great contribution to the field, can be empirically tested and, as we shall see in the next chapter, actually fails the test.

---

[50] The middle term is the term found in both premises, usually the subject of the first premise is the predicate of the second premise, as in example #1

[51] http://en.wikipedia.org/wiki/Chromosome_2_%28human%29 [Accessed April 2012].

[52] IJdo, J. W. et al. 1991. Origin of human chromosome 2: an ancestral telomere-telomere fusion. *Proceedings of the National Academy of Sciences* 88, no. 20: 9051–9055.

[53] This narrow-angle color image of the Earth, dubbed *Pale Blue Dot*, is a part of the first ever portrait of the solar system, taken by *Voyager 1*. The spacecraft acquired a total of 60 frames for a mosaic of the solar system from a distance of more than 4 billion miles from Earth and about 32 degrees above the ecliptic. From Voyager's great distance Earth is a mere point of light, less than the size of a picture element even in the narrow-angle camera. Earth was a crescent only 0.12 pixel in size. Coincidentally, Earth lies right in the center of one of the scattered light rays resulting from taking the image so close to the sun. This blown-up image of the Earth was taken through three color filters -- violet, blue and green -- and recombined to produce the color image. The background features in the image are artifacts resulting from the magnification.

[54] Actually, *Voyager 1* is headed for a flyby of a star called AC +79 3888 in about 40,000 years.

[55] Baraminology is a creationist system that classifies organisms into created kinds, or baramins.

[56] For further treatment of these data, see Meyer, Stephen C. et al. 2007. *Explore Evolution: The Arguments For And Against Neo-Darwinism*. Hill House Publishers.

[57] http://news.harvard.edu/gazette/story/2014/06/reading-shapes/

[58] Cooper, J. 2002. *Of Moths and Men: An Evolutionary Tale*. W.W. Norton & Company.

[59] The retina is often said to be wired backwards because the neurons that convey information from the retina's photoreceptor cells lie between the

receptor cells and the incoming light, thus potentially blocking some light. However, the neurons are transparent and, as far as anyone can tell, block little to no incoming light. In addition, the photoreceptor cells are behind the neurons to place them closer to the blood supply (in the choroid) which is required because of the high metabolism of those cells. In other words, the wiring is "backwards" for a reason and the "backward" wiring has no negative consequences on function.

[60] Any group can, of course, endorse a particular doctrine, but the doctrine is ultimately held by the individual members of the group, or at least the majority of members or the most influential members.

[61] Adapted from http://starwars.wikia.com/

[62] For example: http://whyevolutionistrue.word-press.com/2012/11/29/the-amazing-mimicry-of-frogfish/ [Accessed February 2017].

[63] *Proximal* means closer to the body trunk; *distal* means further from the body trunk.

[64] http://nmhm.washingtondc.museum/collections/hdac/Divergent_Evolution_Development.htm [Accessed 2014, no longer available].

[65] http://www.pbs.org/wgbh/evolution/library/01/4/l_014_01.html [Accessed February 2017].

[66] The *Coelacanth* is the most famous example of a living fossil, but more recently a sulfur bacterium has been discovered that evolutionists claim has not changed in more than 2 billion years: https://phys.org/news/2015-02-scientists-hasnt-evolved-billion-years.html (Accessed January 2017).

[67] Ostrom, J.H. 1975. The Origin of Birds. *Annual Review of Earth and Planetary Sciences* 3:61.

[68] Thulborn, R.A. 1984. The avian relationships of Archaeopteryx, and the origin of birds. *Zoological Journal of the Linnean Society.* 82: 119-158.

[69] Witmer, L.M. 2011. Paleontology: an icon knocked from its perch. *Nature* 475:458-459.

[70] Berra, T. 1990. *Evolution and the Myth of Creationism.* Stanford University Press.

[71] Barras, C. 2014. Missing link fossils may be a jumble of species. New Scientist 2964 (April 12). https://www.newscientist.com/article/mg22229643-200-human-missing-link-fossils-may-be-jumble-of-species/ (Accessed March 2017).

[72] Raven, P., G. Johnson, K. Mason, J. Losos, and S. Singer.2014. *Biology.* (10th ed.). New York: McGraw-Hill.
I reference this textbook several times citing from it examples of evolutionary thinking, but it was chosen at random and any modern biology textbook would present essentially the same material within the same worldview.

[73] Lewis, C.S.1949. Is Theology Poetry. In *The Weight of Glory and Other Addresses*. New York: HarperCollins.

[74] ibid.

[75] Quite obviously, paternity and familial relationships can be established using DNA comparisons. Today, this is even done routinely and cheaply by private companies for curious individuals. However, this is not the nature of the comparisons that evolutionists perform to determine ancestral relationships between individuals from different species who lived millions of years apart. In that case, evolutionists are comparing sections of DNA and assuming that a higher similarity equals a closer relationship. This is fundamentally no different that comparing two skeletons and assuming that a higher degree of similarity equals a closer relationship. The distinction between these two ways of comparing DNA is also briefly described in Section 2.2.1

4

THE TWO PARTS OF EVOLUTION

"Beware false knowledge; it is more dangerous than ignorance."
George Bernard Shaw

Biological evolution can be divided into two basic components: the mythical part and the mechanistic part. By mythical I am referring again to the traditional definition of myth as discussed in chapter 2. Specifically, a myth is a narrative about the origins of the world and humanity that most people assume to be true, and it reveals the deepest values of the culture that espouses it. The mythical part of evolution includes far more than mere "change over time." It is a worldview that includes the origin of the universe (big bang), the origin of the solar system and Earth (coalescence of solar dust), the origin of life (primordial soup), and the origin of man (descent with modification from a universal common ancestor). Biological evolution, strictly speaking, begins with the emergence of the first replicating life form from the primordial soup. All of these various stages of evolution are held to be true by those who espouse them, and they entail a certain value system, e.g., a godless existence, no plan or purpose to life, no essential difference between man and other organisms, etc.

The mechanistic part of evolution deals with *how* evolution happens. Natural selection is the mechanism proposed by Charles Darwin and is considered by his followers to be the primary driving force of evolution.

Although biological evolution is rarely discussed as a two-part stratagem, the two parts have long been recognized. Stephen J. Gould, in his Introduction to *Evolution: The Triumph of an Idea*, puts it this way:

> *"In discussing the truth of evolution, we should make a distinction, as Darwin explicitly did, between the simple fact of evolution – defined as the genealogical connection among all earthly organisms, based on their descent from a common ancestor, and the history of*

any lineage as a process of descent with modification – and theories (like Darwinian natural selection) that have been proposed to explain the causes of evolutionary change."

In other words, we can distinguish the *fact* of evolution from the *mechanism* of evolution, or rather, the myth from the mechanism.

4.1 Evolution: The Mythical Part

The mythical part of evolution is loaded with assumptions and conceptual / philosophical facts. These are swimming in the background of evolutionary thought and are rarely questioned or critically examined. Below are a few of the main assumptions.

4.1.1 The Assumption of Universal Evolutionism

One of the most entrenched and pernicious assumptions in Darwinism is the belief that everything flows naturally through time advancing from the simple to the complex, an idea C.S. Lewis called *universal evolutionism*. Lewis described precisely what he meant:

> *"By universal evolutionism I mean the belief that the very formula of universal process is from imperfect to perfect, from small beginnings to great endings, from rudimentary to the elaborate, the belief which makes people find it natural to think that morality springs from savage taboos... thought from instinct, organic from inorganic. This is perhaps the deepest habit of mind in the contemporary world. It seems to me immensely implausible, because it makes the general course of nature so very unlike those parts of nature we can observe."[76]*

Darwinists may assert that, strictly speaking, natural selection guides organisms to become better fit for their environments, not necessarily "more advanced," but the assertion is disingenuous. The graphical depiction of human evolution – practically a logo for Darwinism – visually captures the unstated assumption of universal evolutionism (Figure 4-1).[77]

As Lewis noted, the general acceptance of this assumption is peculiar since it goes against our every observation of nature. Contrary to the proposition, the observation is a general winding down, a falling apart or wearing out of things; an observation formalized in Newton's second law of thermodynamics.[78] Among living things, universal evolutionism leads one to conclude that new organisms are continually "on the rise" via speciation or adaptation, but the fossil record tells a story of extinction. It is estimated that more than 99% of all species that once inhabited the Earth are now extinct.[79]

The proposition of universal evolutionism is almost certainly an erroneous transposition of mankind's technological progress onto the natural world. Because man's power over nature has so rapidly advanced in recent centuries it is easy to assume that this forward march is the natural progression of everything. But what separates man from nature is *intelligence*. Mankind marches forward, nature just marches on. C. S. Lewis observed: "Believers in progress note that in the world of machines the new model supersedes the old; from this they falsely infer a similar kind of supersession in such things as virtue and wisdom." – and, I might add, biological organisms. But virtue, wisdom, and biological kinds (i.e., baramin) are fixtures in Nature. I wholly agree with the conclusion of Lewis: "The obviousness or naturalness which most people seem to find in the idea of emergent evolution thus seems to be a pure hallucination."

Being that we live in a universe of cause-and-effect, one must also wonder what would be the causative force behind universal evolutionism. Charles Darwin and Charles Lyell proposed that over-reproduction followed by a struggle for limited resources drives evolutionary change in organisms and on its face this appears to be a satisfactory answer. But observation of the real world indicates that most organisms do not over-reproduce – they

Figure 4-1: The standard depiction of human evolution.

produce sufficient numbers for their place on the food chain. The problem of motivation is especially acute when we go all the back to the first emerging cell. All living things possess a will to survive, but what could motivate non-living material to come to life? In his definition of evolution, Jerry Coyne referred to a "self-replicating molecule" (see Section 2.6), but what motivation could a molecule have to self-replicate? What would drive a rock to reproduce itself? What impulse exists that could make a molecule copy itself – whether CO_2, H_2O, $C_6H_{12}O_6$, or a lipid or a protein or DNA? Even within the evolutionary framework, does not replication merely produce competitors? But reproduction is for posterity, it may be argued, for continuance of the species after death of the individual. But why then, as posed in Chapter 1, should non-living matter with the miraculous ability to animate itself not be able to also live forever? From whence comes this process of aging and death?

Darwinists contend that the first life form arose from self-replicating molecules in a primordial soup. One can rightly ask what would drive or motivate such an occurrence. The origin of life and universal evolutionism are just-so stories, not science. Both the mechanism of universal evolutionism and the motives behind it remain a mystery.

4.1.2 The Assumption of Phylogenetic Recapitulation

Another assumption is the pervasive impression that various (and especially more primitive) organisms alive today for some reason hold a resemblance to organisms that lived millions of years ago along the growing branches of the tree of life; a process we might call *phylogenetic recapitulation*. In other words, each successive evolutionary stage of an advanced organism is represented by lesser advanced organisms still in existence. This notion is implied in virtually every discussion of evolutionary intermediates or ancestors, but I have never seen it more openly discussed by anyone than evolutionist and author Neil Shubin in his book, *Your Inner Fish*. On page 10 of his book, Shubin writes:

> "We can make detailed predictions about what the species in each layer [of rock] might actually look like by comparing them with species of animals that are alive today; this information helps us to predict the kinds of fossils we will find in ancient rock layers. In fact,

the fossil sequences in the world's rocks can be predicted by comparing ourselves with animals at our local zoo."

Although evolutionists often rely on this relationship between living and past organisms, there is no reason why such a relationship would exist and nothing in evolution theory even predicts that any such relationship *should* exist. Why should modern animals at the zoo give us any hint whatsoever as to the progression of changes that have occurred over time during the evolution of man (for instance)? And if such a persistent similarity does exist between living organisms and buried fossils does it not immediately suggest that the fossils are actually from deceased modern species or extinct variants?

There is a wide range of variance even within living species today. Take dogs for example. Imagine finding a doggy graveyard filled with skeletons of bulldogs, great Danes, and St. Bernards. Wouldn't it be tempting for a paleontologist to arrange these fossils into some sort of progressive order? Which brings us to the relevance of the fossil record and the assumption of homology.

4.1.3 The Assumption of Homology

Homology is defined by Merriam-Webster as "the likeness in structure between parts of different organisms due to evolutionary differentiation from the same or corresponding part of a remote ancestor." In 1843, sixteen years before Darwin's publication of *Origins*, Richard Owen defined homology simply as "the same organ in different animals." Clearly, the definition of *homology* has evolved. To Darwinists, homologous structures stand in contrast to analogous structures, which are similar structures in organism that did not share a common ancestor. Thus, bat wings and bird wings are analogous structures, but bat wings and human arms are homologous structures.[80] To the creationist, all such structures are analogous (or homologous by Owen's definition) and the modern concept of homology is a fabrication. It is a rather useful fabrication to evolutionists, however, because it reinforces many philosophical / conceptual facts in Darwinism.

When it comes to the fossil record we must first ask: can buried fossils actually even provide a record of biological history? Fossils do not come with labels attached.[81] As pointed out in Section 3.3.8.2, the fact that we can arrange fossilized skeletons into seemingly progressive lineages only demonstrates that the human brain can formulate patterns out of shapes. Fossils do not and cannot show any actual ancestral relationship between organisms. This fact has been conceded by Gareth Nelson, Emeritus Curator at the American Museum of Natural History:

> "The idea that one can go to the fossil record and expect to empirically recover an ancestor-descendant sequence, be it of species, genera, families, or whatever, has been, and continues to be, a pernicious illusion."[82]

Unfortunately, very few other biologists recognize that ancestry derived from the fossil record is true only in the minds of believers. It is another conceptual fact giving rise to coherent truth with no correspondence to objective reality.

Using different year models of corvettes, evolutionist Tim Berra inadvertently illustrated this point (known by creationists as "Berra's blunder") in his book *Evolution and the Myth of Creationism*. The basis of Berra's blunder is that he employs human technological progress and the uniquely human penchant for fashion as an example of Darwinian-style evolution. In other words, he "notes that in the world of machines the new model supersedes the old" and interprets this as evidence for biological evolution.

Berra's blunder in fact illustrates when and where evolution (i.e., change over time) really can occur: only in the minds and products of intelligent beings. Car styles, clothing styles, hair styles, technology, language – these expressions of human thought can and do change over time, or evolve. Living organisms, however, do not. At least not beyond a genetically-determined range of variance.

Although Berra's blunder has received much criticism from advocates of Intelligent Design and creationism, the critiques have not been understood or even acknowledged by evolutionists. Eighteen years after Tim Berra published his book, Neil Shubin repeated Berra's blunder, corvettes and all, on page 106 of his book, *Your Inner Fish*.

Ancestral relationship cannot be definitively established by fossils. Indeed, a relationship cannot even be reasonably inferred by fossils. Imagine finding two fossilized human skeletons in a common grave. You can likely tell by the skeletons whether the dead were male or female, young or old. Even if one skeleton was from an old man and the other from a young man, you cannot tell by skeletons alone if the two are related. Were they father and son, or were they merely friends? Were they enemies? If we cannot determine whether two fossilized human skeletons might be related by a single generation, is it reasonable to conclude we can determine ancestral relationships between different species over millions of years using fossil data? Add to this the alleged phenomena of convergence and divergence (Section 3.3.8.2). If convergence and divergence are true, then fossils cannot in principle distinguish between them.

Before leaving the fossil record, we should remember that *fossil* refers not only to preserved bone but also to mineralized soft structures or the impressions of soft structures in rock. Recognizing this, consider the butterfly. Upon hatching from its egg, the larval caterpillar crawls along the ground and munches on leaves. When ready, the caterpillar seemingly melts into an acorn-like chrysalis from which it emerges as a winged butterfly. The butterfly clumsily flies from flower to flower drinking sugar-rich nectar. If these creatures were extinct and we knew of them only by fossils, would anyone think to connect butterflies with caterpillars? This illustrates yet another limitation of the fossil record.

4.1.4 The Assumption of Uniformitarianism

Catastrophism and uniformitarianism are two proposed mechanisms for how the Earth might change over time. Catastrophism predicts that the Earth remains largely unchanged for long periods of time but can undergo massive changes quickly during bursts of catastrophe. Uniformitarianism predicts that the Earth undergoes drastic changes slowly by the steady hand of natural processes, such as the movements of wind and water and continents. Catastrophic changes can (and have) been observed, but uniformitarianism, like evolution itself, can only be inferred, not observed, because of the requisite time scales. Nonetheless, uniformitarianism is widely embraced by Darwinists today because it coheres with their worldview.

Both mechanisms probably shape the Earth to some degree. Catastrophists certainly recognize the effects of wind and rain and other environmental factors on the landscape of the Earth, but they generally assume these effects are minor and balance out over time such that no significant

Earth-wide changes occur over long periods. Likewise, uniformitarians do recognize that catastrophes happen and can have an enormous influence on the Earth, but a uniformitarian would add that slow, steady changes also take place that lead to equally dramatic – or greater – alterations of the Earth over eons of time and that such processes are most responsible for Earth's present condition.

Most creationists, certainly those of the young Earth variety, are proponents of catastrophism if for no other reason than their acceptance of the Biblical account of a global flood and their rejection of the enormous time scales required for uniformitarianism. In other words, it is coherent with *their* worldview. Evolutionists, on the other hand, believe strongly in uniformitarianism. I say "believe in" because uniformitarianism cannot be observed, only inferred. Indeed, the theory of biological evolution *depends* on slow, gradual processes. So wrote Darwin in *The Origin of Species*: "The old notion that all the inhabitants of the Earth having been swept away by catastrophes at successive periods is generally given up."

Although I'm personally not aware of a single Darwinist who accepts a world-wide flood as a historical fact, evolutionists are willing to embrace catastrophism when it suits them. For example, Carl Zimmer states boldly in his book *Evolution: The Triumph of an Idea*, "Darwin was wrong about extinctions. Catastrophic waves of extinction are a reality. They have ripped through the fabric of life, destroying as many as 90 percent of all species on Earth in a geological instant. The suspects behind these mass extinctions are many, including volcanoes, asteroids, and sudden changes to the oceans and the atmosphere." Indeed, most evolutionists believe the dinosaurs were driven to extinction by the impact of a massive meteor. Evolutionists can accept catastrophism it seems, as long as the catastrophe is not a global flood.

I've already pointed out that uniformitarianism cannot be directly observed whereas catastrophism can be (and has). Indeed, catastrophic modern events have produced in hours what appear to be slow, erosion-type formations. The Milford Lake canyon, for example, was formed in July 1993 when a dam breached, yet it appears to be a canyon carved out over thousands or millions of years.[83] Rapid canyon formation was also observed, along with rapid stratification, after the Mount St. Helens eruption in 1980.[84]

These last several sections dealt with some of the unprovable assumptions undergirding the myth of Darwinism. Next, we will examine the mechanism of evolution and see if it withstands the empirical test.

4.2 Evolution: The Mechanistic Part

Although the supposed historical events of evolution, such as the emergence of the first fish onto dry land, were not observed and cannot be reproduced, the proposed mechanism of evolution can be tested empirically. Herein lies a distinction between creationism and Darwinism. Both versions of history are myths that describe the origin of the world and humanity, but Darwinism has a proposed mechanism.[85] This in fact was Darwin's great contribution to the emerging hypothesis of biological evolution in the mid-1800s. He called his proposal *natural selection*, but does natural selection actually exist and, if so, does it truly work the way Darwin proposed? How can we test it?

When Charles Darwin proposed natural selection as the causative agent for descent with modification, he had no understanding of genetics. He wrote *Origins* in the 1830s and published the book in 1859. It would not be until 1866 before Gregor Mendel worked out the patterns of inheritance and not until 1953 before it was settled that DNA was the genetic material responsible for inheritance. Now that the agent of inheritance and the rules of inheritance are known, we can more fully put Darwin's idea to the empirical test.

In order for natural selection to work we need heritable traits with unlimited variability, beneficial mutations, and a way of selecting for beneficial mutations. Darwinists contend all of these are well-established facts of evolution, but are they objective / empirical facts or conceptual / philosophical facts?

4.2.1 Darwin's Dare

In *The Origin of Species*, Charles Darwin proffered this dare to his critics:

> "If it could be demonstrated that any complex organ existed, which could not possibly have been formed by numerous, successive, slight modifications, my theory would absolutely break down. But I can find no such case."

In other words, if you can prove that evolution cannot happen, then Darwin will concede that evolution does not happen. By taking this position, Darwin flips the scientific enterprise on its head. He places the burden of proof on those who reject his hypothesis. This is not how science is done, and proving a negative is considered impossible without absolute knowledge of the subject matter, which no one possesses on any subject. Nevertheless, experiments can be done and observations can be made to test the mechanism of natural selection and virtually without exception the results do not favor Darwin.

Darwin posed the challenge and more than a century later Michael Behe responded with an observation which, according to Darwin, is tantamount to a proof that biological evolution does not happen. Behe's argument is called *irreducible complexity*.

Much has been written on irreducible complexity, and so I won't rehash it here. I would highly encourage you to read Behe's original argument in his book *Darwin's Black Box: The Biochemical Challenge to Evolution*. In a nutshell, Behe argues that most molecular machines in the cell are built from several distinct components and that if any single component is missing the whole machine will not function. The machine as a whole cannot evolve without the individual components evolving for their final purpose simultaneously and *before* the machine is functional, meaning there's nothing beneficial for nature to select.

Although irreducible complexity is a powerful argument to those leaning towards creationism, it is yet rejected by evolutionists. The most common retort from Darwinists is that the individual components *can* evolve separately for their *own* purposes and then be co-opted for use in a novel machine. "Evolution is a creative scavenger, taking what is available and putting it to new use." Writes Robert L. Dorit in a response article to Behe's hypothesis published in American Scientist.[86] "The Darwinian process... is like a Third World auto mechanic who will get your car running again, but only if parts already lying around can be used for the repair." Dorit goes on to describe, by way of example, an irreducibly complex system used in hindbrain development that was derived from an irreducibly complex system used in insect development. "The [complex] did not evolve to regulate hindbrain development, it was recruited... Design-from-scratch and direct routes are not luxuries afforded to the evolutionary process."

This retort has problems. First, appealing to "parts already lying around" dismisses the origin of these parts. The car parts lying around a garage – even a Third World garage – were designed by engineers with the end-product in mind, a functioning automobile. Second, Dorit avoids explaining how irreducibly complex systems might arise when simply giving an example of one system being co-opted for use somewhere else. Dorit doesn't explain how the irreducibly complex system in insects evolved in the first place, which is the question raised by Behe. Evolutionists claim the parts of an irreducibly complex machine can evolve separately for separate purposes, then mysteriously find each other to form a new machine with a novel function. But I think it is clear to any objective person that this is wishful thinking. I certainly don't know how one would empirically test such a hypothesis. Third, Dorit (like so many other evolutionists) simply personifies evolution while rejecting a Creator God. Dorit calls evolution a "creative scavenger" and likens evolution to an auto mechanic. This is intelligent design.

So, the origin of the original parts, each exquisitely designed for its final function, is left unanswered. Also still unanswered is how the original irreducibly complex system evolved in the first place. Importantly, co-option has never been observed, it can only be inferred. Co-option is a common response to Behe's biochemical challenge, but it is a just-so story, not a hypothesis that can be tested. Like so many other facts for evolution, it is a conceptual / philosophical fact, not an empirical fact.

Finally, Dorit's matter-of-fact attitude that this particular molecular complex "did not evolve to regulate hindbrain development" but was "recruited" from insect development is wholly unjustified. It is one possible conclusion to the observation that the same molecular machine used in insect development is also used in mammalian hindbrain development, but another feasible conclusion can be made by creationists. This attitude and the concomitant language employed by evolutionists is discussed further in Section 5.8.

Darwin's dare refers to "numerous, successive, slight modifications." These days, we are bombarded with a conception (or misconception) of evolution in the media known as *morphing*. Morphing is not the same as evolution, but it provides a compelling visual which no doubt provides the public, especially children, with a method of imagining evolution in action. Morphing in the movies and, sadly, educational propaganda depends entirely on computer animation and photo manipulation. In the real world, the closest we come to morphing is metamorphosis, a process so out-of-reach to biological evolution that, to my knowledge, no attempt has ever been made to explain it by any evolutionist. How a caterpillar could evolve via "successive, slight modifications" the ability to metamorphose into a butterfly is beyond even the imagination of Darwinists.

Only one viable method of generating Darwin's crucial modifications has been proposed: mutation. In order for the modification to be useful, however, the mutation must be beneficial. Is there such a thing as a beneficial mutation?

4.2.2 Beneficial Mutations

Biological evolution by natural selection absolutely depends on "good mutations." That is, the hypothesis depends upon occasional mutations that provide some benefit to an organism above and beyond its unmutated brethren. Like co-option, the concept of a good mutation is appealing but is not actually supported by observation of the real world.

Mutation means a change or alteration in form and function. In our everyday experiences, change can either be good or bad. For example, your favorite restaurant might change their menu, but whether the change is bad or good depends on your particular tastes. Probably, our everyday experience with change makes it easier for us to carry that good-or-bad connotation over to changes in DNA, but observation of real mutations in real DNA does not support the association.

A manuscript may make a better analogy than a menu. In a written manuscript, an intentional change by the author or editor to clarify a sentence is good, but an unintentional and/or random change of letters in the manuscript is bad since it degrades, rather than enhances, the message. Is it conceivable that a random change in a manuscript, such as an altered or deleted word, could somehow *improve* the writing? After all, Darwin is only asking for a rare beneficial event. No matter how much we might wish to imagine it could, inserting random words or letters into a novel with well-developed characters and plots will never make it better. A random change in a novel will not create an improvement in the work.

In his book, *The Blind Watchmaker*, Richard Dawkins attempted something similar to demonstrate how evolution works. He started with a string of 23 random letters and then altered letters in the sentence randomly. A letter became fixed once the "right letter" in the "right place" had been found. It took 43 iterations to convert the random string of letters into the sentence ME THINKS IT IS LIKE A WEASEL.

Like a weasel, indeed. The final sentence (analogous to a biological function) was known in advance and intelligent manipulation was used to get us there. If this is Dawkins' view of evolution, then it's actually an argument for intelligent design or, at best, theistic (i.e., intelligence-driven) evolution.

The analogy of inserting random letters into a novel is almost not even an analogy at all. DNA is literally a code and the genome an instruction manual or blueprint. Inserting random changes into blueprints and manuscripts will never make architects and authors happy. Further, Darwin is really asking for more than merely improvement by mutation in living organisms; the improvement must also be heritable, which places further restrictions on when, where, and how the mutation must occur.

In 2016, a study published in *Nature* shared the results of the largest human gene survey conducted to date. DNA from over 60,000 individuals were surveyed for variations. Considering a minimum of 20,000 genes per individual, this means that at least 1.2 billion genes were compared for variants. The conclusion: the researchers found a lot of variants, nearly one in eight bases; however, not one variant was found that conferred a benefit to any individual. One critical review of the article sums it up like this:

> *"There's plenty of talk about disease. The authors mention "neutral" variants twice. But there are no mentions of beneficial mutations. You can't find one instance of any of these words: benefit, beneficial, fitness, advantage (in terms of mutation), improvement, innovation, invention, or positive selection.*
>
> *"They mention all kinds of harmful effects from most variants: missense and nonsense variants, frameshift mutations, proteins that get truncated on translation, and a multitude of insertions and deletions. Quite a few are known to cause diseases... As for natural selection, the authors do speak of "negative selection" and "purifying selection" weeding out the harmful mutations, but nowhere do they mention anything worthwhile that positive selection appears to be preserving."*[87]

In other words, the take-home message of this massive genetic screening is once again that mutations are bad, not good.

Besides the above real-world observations, the very concept of a good mutation appears to be a tautology. Traits that currently exist, i.e., those traits that survived, are only considered beneficial because they survived. The tautology inherent in the concept of good mutations is almost universally dismissed by Darwinists, as is the fact that no good mutations have ever been observed. Literally millions of mutations have been introduced into organisms as diverse as bacteria, worms, pigs and plants and yet not one wholly beneficial mutation has been found. Darwinists may balk at that statement, but the fact remains that every mutation ever observed or introduced that confers some short-term benefit to the organism also comes with a fitness cost; the mutants are unable to compete with their unmutated brethren.

What about insects that mutate to resist pesticides or bacteria that mutate to resist antibiotics? Aren't these beneficial mutations? In a sense, they are. However, they are not beneficial mutations as envisioned by evolutionists – the type of modifications that morph one species into another over time. They are, in fact, relatively minor alterations in enzymes or other proteins. For example, an antibiotic may function by inhibiting an important bacterial enzyme and thereby shutting down a critical metabolic pathway. Through a "beneficial mutation," the enzyme is altered such that the function of the enzyme remains, but the inhibitor loses its effect. The bacterium thus becomes resistant to the antibiotic. These are the types of observations that make Darwinists salivate, but they are really no different than intelligent antibody production in the mammalian body when challenged with a new antigen. These are abilities existing within living cells that make them somewhat malleable to fluctuating environmental conditions, but they do not constitute evolution in the Darwinian sense, i.e., the cumulative changes that ultimately lead to new a species, genus and family. They are instead preservative mutations that prevent the species from going extinct under certain stressful conditions. And as I mentioned a moment ago, they come with a fitness cost. When the stress is removed, the organisms revert back or are overcome by their wildtype cousins.

Thus, it appears that good mutations as Darwinists envision them do not really exist. Worse, it is entirely possible that such mutations *could* not exist even in principle based on our expanding knowledge of how proteins fold.

In order to be heritable, all mutations must occur in DNA. But in the living organism the mutations are manifested through the protein products encoded in that DNA. Proteins are built from a chain of amino acids. Given the 20 different amino acids used by living organisms, a very small protein just 5 amino acids long could have some 20 x 20 x 20 x 20 x 20 = 3.2 million different amino acid sequences. A chain of 300 amino acids (the size of a typical protein) could thus have 10^{390} possible sequences. This is a staggering number and, as it turns out, only a very small fraction of those sequences will be able to fold into a stable structure. The vast majority of these possible sequences simply do not fold at all. In the past few decades, the determination of protein structures has grown rapidly, but the discovery of new protein folds has declined to zero. According to the two most authoritative protein fold databases (SCOP and CATH), approximately 1,300 unique protein folds have been discovered, but no new fold has been discovered since 2008. It is likely that we've found all of them, a mere 1,300 folds. Multiple folds are often found in a single protein and protein folds can be mixed-and-matched to create different proteins, but the basic number of folds appears to be fixed at about 1,300.

Mutations to the folds do not create new folds, they cause the known folds to unravel. In other words, mutations simply convert a sequence that folds into a sequence that doesn't. All of the functional folds that could exist do exist and mutations only cause injury to those functional folds. This means that a "good mutation" that generates a novel fold or function is highly unlikely to even be possible.

4.2.2.1 Mutations Need Not Apply

The inability to find a good mutation may be inconsequential anyway since evolution apparently doesn't need mutations in order to march forward. In his book, *The Evolutionary Biology of Human Female Sexuality*, Randy Thornhill writes:

> "New traits are often thought to originate through chance mutation – which, if the manifested trait is selected, can be thought of as a fortuitous mutation. In fact, however, this view is incomplete at best and, in worst cases, simply wrong... The origin of a phenotypic trait

*on the Tree of Life is caused ultimately by the incidental develop-
mental transformation of an ancestral, pre-existing phenotype."*

Unfortunately, this argument does not advance our understanding of
the origin of new phenotypic traits because the origin of the pre-existing
phenotype is not explained, nor is it recognized that phenotype is based on
genotype, nor is the cause or mechanism of the "incidental transformation"
explained.[88] Using the origin of mammary glands as an example, Thornhill
continues:

> *"In the ancestral species in which primordial mammary glands
> arose, sweat glands were the typical end results of a particular de-
> velopmental process. This process... was **somehow transformed**
> such that a novel phenotype, a primordial mammary gland, arose."
> (Emphasis added).*

The express purpose of Thornhill's book is to explain the evolutionary
development of human female sex organs and behavior. Postulating that
mammary glands arose by being *"somehow transformed"* from sweat glands
seems less than satisfactory, especially when arguing that mutations are not
required. Yet this sort of meaningless babble is routinely proffered by evolutionists as science – the only science, by the way, your children are allowed
to learn.

The tone used by Thornhill and other evolutionists is worth noting. In
his description of mammary gland evolution, Thornhill speaks declaratively
and factually, adding a sufficient dose of scientific lingo to give the story an
air of authority, yet he describes nothing. He could be describing the turbo
encabulator.[89] In truth, his tale is wholly speculative. It is nothing more than
a just-so story. But it is not unusual for evolutionists to present speculation
and conjecture as scientific fact. To be fair, these *are* facts in their minds. I
have more to say on the tone used by evolutionists in Section 5.8.

4.2.3 Selecting for Beneficial Mutations (Natural Selection)

Darwin proposed that minor changes in organisms could spontaneously
arise and that nature could preferentially select the fittest members of a
population. As the proposed mechanism of evolution, natural selection gave

teeth to the concept of descent with modification. But is natural selection an empirical fact? Does nature select?

Natural selection is defined by Merriam-Webster as follows: "A natural process that results in the survival and reproductive success of individuals or groups best adjusted to their environment and that leads to the perpetuation of genetic qualities best suited to that particular environment." This is a poor definition. Indeed, the dictionary does not actually define or even attempt to describe the *process* at all but rather skips immediately to the end results of the process. It's like describing the manufacture of a car as a process that *results in* an automobile that can be propelled by combustion, steered with a steering wheel, and stopped by brakes. All of that is true of automobiles, but that does not describe the manufacturing process of the car. We are still left wondering: how is the car actually *built*? In the case of natural selection, what is the actual *process* of natural selection? How does natural selection actually *work*?

According to Biology-Online, perhaps a more authoritative voice on the subject, natural selection is defined this way:

> "A process in nature in which organisms possessing certain genotypic characteristics that make them better adjusted to an environment tend to survive, reproduce, increase in number or frequency, and therefore, are able to transmit and perpetuate their essential genotypic qualities to succeeding generations. It is the process by which heritable traits that increase an organism's chances of survival and reproduction are favored more than less beneficial traits. Originally proposed by Charles Darwin, natural selection is the process that results in the evolution of organisms."

According to both sources, natural selection is a *process*, i.e., a series of actions or operations leading to a particular end product. In this case, the process is conducted by nature as opposed to a manufacturing process, for example, conducted by humans or robots. Since the Biology-Online definition actually describes this process, let's unpack their definition.

In the first clause we read: "A process in nature in which organisms possessing certain genotypic characteristics that make them better adjusted to an environment tend to survive, reproduce, increase in number or frequency." This implies that not all individuals are born equal; some are "better adjusted" to their environment than others. Which organisms are better adjusted? Those that survive. Which organisms survive? Those that are better adjusted. This is a logical fallacy called circular reasoning. Why or how are the individuals not equal? They possess "certain genotypic characteristics" that must differ. How are they made to differ? This is not explained in the definition (because it is beyond the scope of the definition), but ultimately we must know in order for the definition to be meaningful. There are two sources for different genotypes: variations known as gene alleles (such as for blue eyes or brown eyes) and mutation. The alleles provide a fixed range of diversity but mutation can produce unlimited diversity (say evolutionists). We have seen already that beneficial mutations do not exist and we will see in Section 4.2.4 that unlimited variability doesn't either, but let's assume they do for the moment and continue unpacking this definition.

Organisms that are "better adjusted to an environment" are those that survive and reproduce. Therefore, the definition in fact states: "A process in nature in which organisms possessing certain genotypic characteristics that make them [survive and reproduce] tend to survive, reproduce, increase in number or frequency." This is a tautology; the definition simply repeats itself using different words. The increase in number or frequency must be referring to the offspring of the organisms possessing the certain (favorable) genetic characteristics. In nature, we observe that environments provide checks-and-balances to keep populations under control. It could be proposed that an organism might acquire a new trait that allows it to thwart the checks-and-balances resulting in rapid population growth. This has not been observed in nature, however. We have observed populations explode when organisms are moved by humans to a new environment devoid of the checks-and-balances (e.g., the rabbit population in Australia and the kudzu in North America). Also, humans may suppress populations (via pesticides or antibiotics, for example) and organisms have been observed to overcome those suppressive efforts, but that is not quite the same thing.

Returning to our definition of natural selection by Biology-Online, the second part of the first sentence reads: "and therefore, are able to transmit and perpetuate their essential genotypic qualities to succeeding generations." Since the clause begins with "therefore" it is clearly a conclusion. Let us attempt to restate the definition in a syllogistic argument form:

1. Organisms that are better adjusted to their environment survive and reproduce.

2. Organisms that survive and reproduce have essential genotypic qualities.

Therefore, [organisms that survive and reproduce] are able to transmit and perpetuate their essential genotypic qualities to succeeding generations.

To "transmit and perpetuate their essential genotypic qualities to succeeding generations" is the very definition of *reproduce*. Therefore, the conclusion states: Organisms that survive and reproduce are able to survive and reproduce. Another tautology.

Recall that premise 1 already contains our first tautology: Organisms better adjusted to their environment = organisms that survive and reproduce. So premise 1 actually states: Organisms that survive and reproduce, survive and reproduce. Premise 2 states that organisms that survive and reproduce have essential genetic qualities allowing them to survive and reproduce. So the conclusion is that organisms that survive and reproduce are able to survive and reproduce to pass on their genes to progeny that can survive and reproduce.

The only meaningful statement in the argument appears to be premise 2: Organisms that are better adjusted to their environment, i.e., organisms that survive and reproduce, have essential genotypic qualities. This is a true statement, but it is not a process or a mechanism for biological evolution. Indeed, given the observation that the wild type organism is always the best adjusted to survive and reproduce, it follows that the wild type traits are the essential genotypic traits. This conclusion supports the actual role of natural selection which is to maintain biological stasis, not drive biological change (described fully below).

The second sentence of the Biology-Online definition reads: "It is the process by which heritable traits that increase an organism's chances of survival and reproduction are favored more than less beneficial traits." This is merely a rephrasing of the first tautology and actually provides no new information. Favorable traits increase an organisms chances of survival and chances of survival are increased by favorable traits.

In addition to the logical fallacies presented above, it appears that missing from both definitions of natural selection is a requirement that organisms produce significantly more offspring than can survive to reproductive age. This was a crucial part of the definition to Darwin. This assumption, however, is easily challenged (see Section 4.2.6).

The proposal that natural selection is the engine that drives evolution is an appealing hypothesis. It is simple, apparently logical at first glance, and powerful enough to explain how biological evolution could occur. In short, it is *elegant*. The only problem is that the argument is fraught with fallacies, depends entirely on non-existent beneficial mutations and an inferred unlimited diversity, and is wholly unsupported by observations of the real world.

4.2.3.1 The Actual Role of Natural Selection

In the real world, natural selection – divorced from mythical good mutations and logical fallacies – is not an erroneous idea. It is real and has a profound impact on the living world. But if natural selection does not drive evolution what does it do? Ironically, it maintains biological stasis. The true role of natural selection has been turned on its head by Darwinists.

Based on the real-world observation that all mutations are detrimental (or silent, but they can be ignored), it follows that all mutant organisms are less fit for survival, in some small or big way, than their wild type cousins. Survival-of-the-fittest is a real phenomenon, but the fittest are always the wild type organisms according to all our observations. Natural selection acts, therefore, to eliminate the mutants from the population and thereby preserve the original archetype. Seen in this light, which is fully supported by observation, natural selection is a pruning force for maintaining stasis, not fostering change. It is indeed a powerful preservative force but is utterly impotent at driving the supposed continual march from primitive to advanced. It should be noted that artificial selection is a man-made suspension of natural selection which does in fact produce extremely variable offspring – within limits.

The actual role of natural selection is unexciting, even boring compared to the creative function Darwinists imagine. Countless times everyday mutants are quietly pruned from the gene pool by natural selection. Scientists, however, in a desperate bid to advance Darwinism, have spent millions of dollars (and hours) searching for that elusive beneficial mutation. They have not found it. But when they find something close it makes a splash in the headlines and everyone feels their worldview is vindicated. The public is never told that those beneficial mutations come with a fitness cost and are always loss-of-information mutations. No gain-of-information mutation has ever been observed in nature or a lab.

Strictly speaking, natural selection preserves the fittest organisms and is not concerned with whether the species is changing or remaining the same, but since the fittest organism is usually the wild type, stasis is the result. In a few rare cases mutants have been preserved as the fittest, but these are always loss-of-function mutants, never gain-of-function mutants. For example, there are deep-sea fishes that have eyes but have apparently lost their vision, which is unnecessary in the blackness of the ocean depths.

Despite the failure of natural selection to invoke change in the real biological world, the idea is so powerful that it has become fully entrenched in Western thought. For example, natural selection, or rather the logic of natural selection, appeared before me in the most unlikely of places while vacationing in the Outer Banks of North Carolina.

4.2.3.2 The Logic of Natural Selection Goes Beyond Nature

In North Carolina, "First in Flight" is the motto imprinted on their license plates. North Carolinians are right to be proud of the accomplishments of Orville and Wilbur Wright on the shores of Kill Devil Hills. A museum and memorial now mark the spot where the Wright brothers flew the world's first airplane in 1903. I was a bit shocked, however, to read these words in a brochure provided by the Wright Brothers museum:

> *"Any aircraft design has to solve three critical problems: lift – generating an upward force greater than the weight of the plane; thrust – propelling the plane forward; and control – stabilizing and directing the plane's flight. Any number of approaches can achieve these results, but natural selection eliminated the early designs that failed to meet the requirements of efficiency, reliability and durability. The design rapidly evolved into the familiar basic configuration that virtually all airplanes share."[90]*

I have a number of objections to this paragraph in the Wright Brothers brochure.

First, Nature eliminated nothing with respect to airplane design, aeronautical engineers did.

Second, any number of designs *cannot* achieve flight, only a very limited number of designs can, which is why virtually all airplanes share the same "basic configuration." This is another example of the Structure-Function Principle.

Third, airplane designs "evolved" (i.e., changed over time) as human engineers discovered new principles of flight through experimentation and applied those principles to produce configurations which best achieved lift, propulsion, and control. In other words, engineers continued to discover the best structural designs to achieve the desired function — controlled flight.

Obviously nature had nothing to do with the creation of airplanes and airplanes "evolved" only in the sense that intelligent humans learned how to make better airplanes over time. But the idea that things should naturally flow from primitive to complex is so ingrained in us — despite all evidence to the contrary — that it pops up even in a brochure on airplanes.

4.2.4 Unlimited Variability

Artificial selection has been used as an argument for evolution since Darwin himself, but far from demonstrating an open-ended nature for genetic variation, artificial selection actually reveals the limits of genetic variance within a species. Looking to our best friends, dogs, we see that centuries of breeding have produced an enormous variety of canines, but they are all still canines. No one has been able to breed out a new, distinct species from the dogs. The same can be said for every other animal and plant that people have bred. Wide variety can almost always be achieved but never the type of macro-evolutionary changes that turn fish into land animals.

Charles Darwin wrote: "I can see no limit to the amount of change… which may have been effected in the long course of time through nature's power of selection." Evolutionists such as Neil Shubin claim that natural selection can realize in ten or twenty million years what human breeders cannot do over centuries. Creationists say that Shubin and Darwin are guilty of faulty extrapolation (see Section 3.3.3) and that the limits to variability are real and those limits have been reached by breeders. Adding more time to the equation will not overcome this fundamental reality.

Whereas artificial selection creates diversity (within limits), natural selection produces uniformity and stasis. The various breeds of dogs from Great Danes to miniature Chihuahuas have been produced and maintained by artificial selection. Remove man from the equation and within a few generations nature would have all dog breeds revert back to the original, wild dog archetype. These are the limits of variability and the true nature of natural selection.

4.2.5 Some Variation is Apparent

Having explained the limits of variability and the main role of natural selection, I would now like to back-peddle just a little. Although it appears that variation in organisms is not unlimited, there is obviously *some* variation available, mainly through gene variations called alleles.[91] This variability is allowed to express itself in different environments and it may be concluded that Nature, i.e., natural selection, drives the expression of this variability. It seems reasonable that leopards, tigers, lions, and even domestic cats belong to a single created kind, or baramin. Yet the *Felidae* baramin has enough built-in variability to allow the separation of these distinct sub-kinds, or species, in different environments. Thus, natural selection may contribute to variability within a baramin, but this is an inferred conclusion. Importantly, natural selection is powerless to convert one kind into another. Thus, the Darwinian Tree of Life may be accurate above the "creationist line" (depicted as the dashed line in Figure 4-2), but it seems apparent that diversification by natural selection cannot be extrapolated below that line.

Whether or not natural selection creates diversity above the creationist line, it's important to remember that natural selection is not an objective fact. It is process, or event. Indeed, it is a *conceptual* event (see Section 2.2.1) because it has never been observed. It is inferred largely from artificial selection, which *has* been observed and is thus an objective / empirical event.

4.2.6 Is There a Struggle for Resources?

In formulating the concept of natural selection Darwin drew upon a proposition by Thomas Malthus that more organisms – many more – are born than can possibly survive to adulthood to reproduce. They all cannot survive, according to Malthus, because of limited resources. Today, we often accept this proposition as a given, but is it an empirical fact? It appears to be true for some species, but certainly not for all. Consider the following observations:

- One nest of 2,000 frog eggs may produce only 5-10 adult frogs.
- The wild African dog will produce 5-10 pups per year for roughly her 10 reproductive years, or 50-100 dogs.
- The female African elephant will produce only about 4 offspring during her 60-year lifespan.

Malthus and Darwin proposed that organisms produce far more offspring than will possibly survive and that nature selects only the fittest for survival to reproductive age. However, based on the above observations, it appears that the number of offspring produced by an organism is correlated roughly with its position on the food chain. Most organisms that reproduce

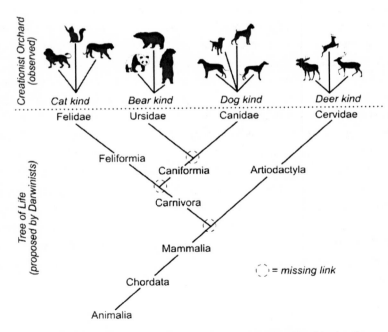

Figure 4-2: The Orchard of Life and the creationist line (dashed).

in the thousands only to obtain a few adults are killed by predation, not limited resources. Darwin and Malthus seem to be applying observations made for some organisms (like tadpoles) to all of biology, which is clearly erroneous. In addition, many factors contribute to death and/or survival rates, most of which appear to be random.

Finally, according to the principles of evolution, organisms that reproduce prolifically and with short generation times should evolve at a faster rate than organisms with long lifespans and few offspring, yet there's no empirical evidence to support that prediction. Indeed, based on Darwinian logic it follows that insects, amphibians, fish, and bacteria should be among the most highly evolved organisms on Earth, with elephants and humans among the least evolved. Some Darwinists sarcastically suggest that insects and germs are more highly evolved than humans and that's a topic discussed in Section 5.7. Seriously though, Darwinists claim that insects and germs are suitably, perhaps maximally or perfectly, evolved for their niche in the environment, but this is a philosophical position. Creationists would agree that all organisms are perfectly adapted for their niches, just as God made them to be.

4.2.7 Putting It All Together

In a 2015 article, evolutionist Charlie Martin put the elements discussed in the above sections together into one long and subtle slight-of-hand.[92] Martin lists the necessities of biological evolution and marks each item on the list as fact or inference. He draws upon a summary of Darwinism by Ernst Meyer that goes as follows:

1. Every species is fertile enough that if all offspring survived to reproduce the population would grow (claimed as fact).
2. Despite periodic fluctuations, populations remain roughly the same size (claimed as fact).
3. Resources such as food are limited and are relatively stable over time (claimed as fact).
4. A struggle for survival ensues (claimed as inference).
5. Individuals in a population vary significantly from one another (claimed as fact).
6. Much of the variation is heritable (claimed as fact).

7. Individuals less suited to the environment are less likely to survive and less likely to reproduce; individuals more suited to the environment are more likely to survive and more likely to reproduce and leave their heritable traits to future generations (claimed as inference)

8. This slowly effected process results in populations changing to adapt to their environments, and ultimately, these variations accumulate over time to form new species (claimed as inference).

Obviously, it is my opinion that the Darwinian conclusion from the above list of observations and inferences is incorrect, but I also take issue with some of the above points being claimed as facts. For instance, without using circular reasoning, what exactly is a "significant" variation claimed in point #5? And are resources truly a limiting factor in controlling most populations, as claimed in point #3? As explained in the previous section, most rabbits die from predators, not a lack of resources. Most fish die from predators, not a lack of resources. Thus, the predator-prey balance, rather than lack of resources, seems to maintain at least some, if not most, population sizes.

And this brings us to the inferences found in points #7 and #8. Is it true that individuals can escape predation if they possess certain traits that their kin are lacking? Can they acquire changes (i.e., mutations) that benefit them? As described already, despite their powerful appeal, beneficial mutations do not exist; at least, none have been observed. All observed mutations negatively impact the organism or have no impact. Those impacted with mutations may fall more readily to a predator, and this fulfills the real purpose of natural selection – to weed out the mutants and maintain the integrity of the gene pool. Since no new useful genetic information can be added by mutation and natural selection maintains genomic stasis (point #7), Darwinian speciation or the emergence of new genera or families (point #8) does not occur in the real world. Discounting the effects of natural selection to weed out the mutant, death by accident or predation is random.

Martin apparently fails to realize that actual observation of the natural world indicates natural selection (point #7) maintains constancy in a species over time because all observed mutations are negative or neutral. The natural reversion of man-made variants to their archetype is further evidence to this point. To help explain his view of natural selection, Martin used the following analogy:

Martin has us imagine a coin toss with 1000 coins. All coins that land heads-up survive, but those that land tails-up die. After the first toss, 500 coins will land heads-up. After the next toss, 250 coins will land heads-up. "But now," writes Martin, "let's slip in some ringers, unfair coins: some always come up heads... Eventually, if you flip the coins long enough there will be nothing left but the all-heads ringers. That's natural selection."

Unfortunately for evolutionists, that's not reality. The all-heads ringers represent individuals with those magical beneficial mutations and unlimited variability. They do not exist.

Martin also claims that this notion of natural selection is falsifiable and has passed the test:

> "If species arise through natural selection, you would expect all the examined species to form a single phylogenetic tree, or at most a very few trees. So, to falsify the notion that natural selection leads to new species, you would examine the genomes of a lot of organisms. If they don't form a clean tree that would seem to falsify this notion of natural selection."

First, Martin's logic is not sound because a phylogenetic Tree of Life constructed of shared traits is derived from the Structure-Function Principle, not ancestry. Second, the Darwinian Tree of Life presented in textbooks is a complete fabrication. Every branch point is an unobserved intermediate – a proposed link that is missing. The actual observation from nature is an orchard, not a tree (Figure 4-2). Most lineages arise independently and very quickly in what is known as the Cambrian Explosion. By Martin's logic, this should be taken as clear evidence discounting natural selection. Third, Martin is using inference not experiment, so the argument is not empirically falsifiable despite his claim. This is a textbook example of confusing paradigm-dependent affirmation by inference for actual empirical data. Remember the admonition by Francisco Ayala in Section 2.1.1:

> "If a hypothesis is formulated to account for some known phenomena, these phenomena may provide credibility to the hypothesis, but by themselves do not amount to a genuine empirical test of it for the purpose of validating it."

Once again, we find that evolution is a house of cards propped up not by empirical evidence but by philosophical / conceptual facts that are merely coherent with the Darwinist's worldview.

76 Lewis, C.S. 1949. *The Weight of Glory and Other Addresses*. New York: HarperCollins.

77 iStock.com/Man_Half-tube.

78 It is true that living systems evade entropy to remain alive, but that evasion is achieved by the overall increase of disorder in the environment via ingestion and metabolism for animals and, for photosynthetic organisms, by capturing the energy released by the diminishment of the sun.

79 Stearns, B.P. and S.C. Stearns. 2000. *Watching, from the Edge of Extinction*. Yale University Press., pg.1921.

80 According to Darwinists, all living things have evolved from a single common ancestor, thus all structures are ultimately homologous. "Though bird and bat wings are analogous as wings, as forelimbs they are homologous. Birds and bats did not inherit wings from a common ancestor with wings, but they did inherit forelimbs from a common ancestor with forelimbs." http://evolution.berkeley.edu/evolibrary/article/evo_09 [Accessed June 2016].

81 Pritchard, T. How can all the scientists be wrong? http://www.creationstudies.org/Education/How%20can%20all%20the%20scientists%20be%20wrong.pdf [Accessed January 2017].

82 Williams, D. M. and M. C. Ebach. 2004. The reform of palaeontology and the rise of biogeography--25 years after 'ontogeny, phylogeny, palaeontology and the biogenetic law (Nelson, 1978). *Journal of Biogeography* 31: 685-712.

83 Wolfrom, G. W. 1994. The 1993 midwest floods and rapid canyon formation. *Creation Research Society Quarterly* 31(2):109. http://www.creationresearch.org/crsq/articles/31/31_2b/31_2b.html

84 Austin, S. A. 1986. Mt. St. Helens and Catastrophism. *Acts & Facts*. 15 (7). http://www.icr.org/article/mt-st-helens-catastrophism/

85 The lack of a mechanism for divine creation, other than "God spoke and – Bang! – it happened," is perhaps a major reason why creationism is rejected by so many scientists. But the lack of a mechanism does not weaken the hypothesis with respect to historical investigation, only with respect to empirical investigation. And as we see in Section 4.2, much of the evidence for natural selection, the proposed mechanism for evolution, still relies on inference. When it can be tested empirically, it fails virtually every test.

[86]Dorit, R.L. 1997. A Review of *Darwin's Black Box: The Biochemical Challenge to Evolution*, by Michael J. Behe. American Scientist (September-October) http://www.americanscientist.org/bookshelf/pub/a-review-of-darwins-black-box-the-biochemical-challenge-to-evolution-by-michael-j-behe [Accessed January 2017].

[87]A Billion Genes and Not One Beneficial Mutation. http://www.evolutionnews.org/2016/08/a_billion_genes103091.html [Accessed January 2017].

[88] Genotype is the DNA sequence for a gene; phenotype is the trait revealed by expression of the gene.

[89] The turbo encabulator is a fictitious engine humorously described as a real device. https://www.youtube.com/watch?v=rLDgQg6bq7o

[90] Wright Brothers National Memorial Official Map and Guide. National Park Service, U.S. Dept. of Interior. Reprinted 2002.

[91] Virtually every definition of *allele* attributes mutation to their existence, but this is an inference. It is just as possible that God simply created different versions of some genes to allow variability (e.g., eye color).

[92] Martin, C. 2015. Is the Science Ever Settled? Theories, Hypotheses, and What Science Really Does. http://pjmedia.com/blog/is-the-science-ever-settled-theories-hypotheses-and-what-science-really-does/ [Accessed January 2017].

5

BEYOND BIOLOGY

"A man sees in the world what he carries in his heart."
Van Goethe

5.1 Astronomer Carl Sagan

Due largely to the influence of Darwin's theory, most biologists have adopted a wholly naturalistic worldview; that is, an atheistic worldview, at least with respect to origins. Other hard sciences, such as chemistry and physics and astronomy, have been slower to succumb to naturalistic materialism, though it has been creeping into those fields at a growing rate. Even today, many astronomers remain theists,[93] but since astronomy has provided some of the strongest evidence for an ancient universe this branch of science has bolstered the hypothesis of biological evolution in recent decades despite still operating principally on hard, empirical data.

The late Carl Sagan is one of the most famous champions of Darwinism in the last century, but Sagan was not a biologist. He was an astronomer who applied the "logic of Darwinism" (see Section 5.3) to astronomy. He demonstrates that the appeal of Darwinism reaches far beyond the realm of biology. Indeed, Darwinism now permeates nearly every aspect of our culture and this may be a clue that Darwinism is something other than empirical science.

Carl Sagan searched endlessly for extraterrestrial life. Finding none, he once marveled at the *Voyager 1* photograph shown in Figure 3-4. He waxed poetic about our Pale Blue Dot with these words:

> *"From this distant vantage point the Earth might not seem of any particular interest, but for us... that's here. That's home. That's us. On it everyone you love, everyone you know, everyone you ever heard of, every human being who ever was, lived out their lives... on a mote of dust suspended in a sunbeam."[94]*

His Darwinist worldview becomes apparent as he continues:

"Our posturings, our imagined self-importance, the delusion we have some privileged position in the universe are challenged by this point of pale light. Our planet is a lonely speck in the great, enveloping cosmic dark. In our obscurity, in all this vastness, there is no hint that help will come from elsewhere to save us from ourselves."

This is the message heard by every schoolchild in America's public schools since the Scopes Monkey Trial.[95] Carl Sagan's documentary, *Cosmos: A Personal Voyage*, has been watched by millions of children in science classrooms in the past four decades. Gone is any reference to the help that did come: "For God so loved the world that he gave his only Son, that whoever believes in him should not perish but have eternal life." (John 3:16).

5.2 Physicist Brian Cox

The late astronomer Carl Sagan led the move among astronomers to adopt the Darwinists' worldview, but many other astronomers have followed suit. Brian Cox, a senior scientist for the Large Hadron Collider (LHC), exemplifies the astronomer of the new school.

The LHC is an enormous 17-mile long tunnel in which protons are accelerated to very near the speed of light and then slammed into each other. Using such instruments scientists have been able to break apart subatomic particles and examine their constituent parts. A 16-minute video of Brian Cox explaining the LHC at a 2008 TED conference is available on YouTube.[96] In the first ten minutes of this video Cox makes no less than nine references to "looking into the past" or "back in time" or peering into the very "beginning of the universe." The last several minutes of the video is devoted entirely to the telling of this new, secular creation story, the "scientific creation story" Cox calls it.

Why does Cox insist that by slamming high-speed protons into each other we are studying the origin of the universe? By slamming protons together at high speed aren't we studying, well, what happens when you slam protons together at high speed? Maybe this does mimic the conditions of the universe 10^{-9} second after it was born, or maybe it doesn't.

Incidentally, Cox goes on to say in the 2008 TED lecture, "[The fact] that civilization, which if you believe the scientific creation story, has emerged purely from the laws of physics and a few hydrogen atoms... makes me feel incredibly valuable." How this makes him feel valuable is beyond me. Neil Shubin, Richard DeWitt, and other evolutionists have made similar metaphysical / spiritual comments (see Section 5.7). Why do scientists discussing hard science inject these philosophical viewpoints into their discussions? Because they understand the human need for meaning, and they must imagine that meaning can be found in a "cold, old universe" (as Cox puts it) apart from a mindful, purposeful, Creator God.

To observe elementary particles emerging from annihilated protons in the LHC is science. To assert – as a matter of fact – that this replicates conditions that existed 14 billion years ago when the entire universe was supposedly smaller than an atom is at best a hypothesis, more loosely speculation, and in truth borders on science fiction. To talk about it all making you "feel incredibly valuable" is blatantly unscientific.

5.3 Physicist Lee Smolin

A number of books on evolution are worthless for actually learning about Darwin's theory, like *Evolution: The Triumph of an Idea*. It is essentially one long fairy-tale. Much of what author Carl Zimmer writes is so fantastical that you must constantly remind yourself that he is not intentionally writing science fiction. Likewise, the collection of essays in *Intelligent Thought: Scientists versus the Intelligent Design Movement*, edited by John Brockman, are not particularly good resources for understanding biological evolution *per se*, but they are highly informative for exposing how Darwinists think. Reading the book one gets the image of good 'ole boys smoking cigars and slapping each other on the back while scoffing at their creationist enemies. Each author takes Darwinian evolution as a given and then throws hapless punches at creationists or delves off into flights of fancy on how evolution might explain this or that complex phenomenon (like morality). The chapter by Lee Smolin entitled "Darwinism All the Way Down" is particularly rich in Darwinian phantasm.

In his chapter, Smolin – a physicist – argues that the laws of nature have and continue to evolve via a Darwinian mechanism. He explicitly claims that "there is indeed a multiverse consisting of a population of universes that are related to one another *genetically* – that is each universe, including our own, has ancestors and progeny." (Emphasis added). I'm not sure where this physicist studied genetics, but I'm quite certain it's impossible for universes to be genetically related. (A *gene*, according to Merriam-Webster, is "a specific sequence of nucleotides in DNA or RNA that is located usually on a chromosome."), but let's give Smolin the benefit of the doubt and assume he's using the word "genetically" in the broadest possible sense, meaning one universe can somehow produce progeny, or subsequent universes.

Let's take a closer look at Smolin's proposition. He asks how we can obtain a biofriendly universe like ours so highly attuned in its physical parameters to support life without appealing to an anthropic principle. His answer is "to construct a multiverse theory within which our universe is a typical member of a highly non-random population, rather than an improbable member of a random population."

"How are we to do this?" Smolin asks. "The only way I know is to... extend the *logic of Darwinism* to the universe and the laws of physics." (Emphasis added). Smolin continues:

> "To apply the logic of natural selection to cosmology, one needs the following elements:
>
> (1) A process by which universes reproduce themselves
>
> (2) A process by which the parameters of the standard model of particle physics change by small, random increments in each new universe produced. These first two elements result in a population of universes with a distribution of parameters.
>
> (3) A mechanism of selective pressure that will result in a highly non-random distribution of parameters. This happens if the number of progeny a universe has is strongly dependent on the choices of parameters.
>
> Unlike the hypotheses involving... anthropic principles, [the above] hypothesis can result in a theory that is falsifiable by observations – because the population of universes created by a process of natural selection will be far from random. Our universe will then be seen as a typical member of this very untypical collection of universes."

So, what observations can we make to falsify Smolin's theory? How do we put it to the test? Smolin claims, "What we need to determine, in order to test the theory, is only that *almost* every other universe in the *collection* has a *property not required for our existence*." (Emphases added).

One, what does "almost" mean when testing a scientific hypothesis? Two, how do we compare a "collection" of universes when the only one we can observe is our own? (And for all we know is the only one that exists). And, three, is simply finding a "property not required for our existence" sufficient to validate such a theory? The only "observable" piece of evidence Smolin provides is black holes, by which universes allegedly reproduce. Since physicists believe black holes can only form in a universe with carbon and oxygen, Smolin concludes: "a biofriendly universe is also a black-hole-friendly universe! Universes that aren't biofriendly won't have black holes, and therefore the biofriendly ones predominate." This is supposedly the evidence for proposition (3), but it seems that only a universe exactly like ours, with our finely-tuned parameters, is capable of producing oxygen and carbon at all. In any case, how would you know there are many universes *sort of* like ours with oxygen and carbon?

Proposition (2) requires a process by which the parameters of nature change by small, random increments. What is the proposed mechanism? It is one by John Archibald Wheeler called "reprocessing the universe" suggested to occur when a new universe in born. What is the evidence for this process? None.

The evidence for proposition (1) – that universes reproduce – is black holes. However, that is pure speculation; a hypothesis we cannot test or confirm.

Smolin assures us that his hypothesis is "falsifiable by observation." Hardly. What experiment does he propose to put his hypothesis to the test? None. What observation can be made that proves our universe is just one of many? None. The entire hypothesis stands only upon the "logic of Darwinism." The picture these men are painting is so fantastical that I can hardly remain polite when they call themselves scientists. The entire scenario is pure conjecture and cannot be tested empirically. At least Smolin does acknowledge, "The evidence I mentioned is, however, theoretical." Or. that we can agree. A theory supported entirely by theoretical evidence.

By the way, certainly not all physicists believe in multiple universes. Paul Davies, a physicist who has written numerous books on physics and God, sees it clearly:

"Not everybody is happy with the many-universes theory. To postulate an infinity of unseen and unseeable universes just to explain the one we do see seems like a case of excess baggage carried to the extreme. It is simpler to postulate one unseen God. Scientifically the many-universes theory is unsatisfactory because it could never be falsified: what discoveries would lead a many-worlder to change his/her mind?"

None.

5.4 Physicist Lisa Randall

In *Intelligent Thought*, Lisa Randall is another physicist arguing the factually of biological evolution. In her chapter "Designing Worlds" she states: "The *mechanism* of evolution is a subject of ongoing research, but the *fact* of evolution has been pretty definitely established." (Emphases in original). Note the two parts of evolution are recognized by Randall. It seems to me, however, that the hypothesis of biological evolution cannot be divorced from its mechanism without becoming a chimera, or science fiction. Warp drives are common in science fiction films but without a real-world mechanism for achieving faster-than-light space travel the concept will remain only in the movies. Likewise, the "fact" of biological evolution stands or falls on the viability of a real-world mechanism for changing real organisms over time. Without a viable mechanism, the inferences regarded as evidence for Darwinism become considerably weaker. According to Randall: "The evidence for the fact of evolution includes the fossil record, which reveals gross characteristics that overlap but are not identical and genetic frequency counts that are similar but not the same." I've already addressed the fossil record (Sections 4.1.3 and 3.2), and "genetic frequency counts that are similar but not the same" is frankly just prattle. Randall continues: "There is concrete evidence for speciation – as evidenced by Darwin's finches on the Galapagos Islands."

There are 15 species of finches on the Galapagos Islands. They were there before scientists came to study them, and they are still there today. Contrary to Randall's assertion, no new species have arisen during that time. Indeed, the 15 species that are on the islands are not even distinct species at all since they can interbreed.[97] There have been reports of small changes in beak size for some species during periods of drought, but the changes have been minor and cyclical – not a continuous small-scale-leading-to-big-scale change the theory demands. Also, as mentioned in Section 3.3.3, a newer study demonstrates there are definite limits to finch beak morphology. In other words, the Galapagos finches do not provide "concrete evidence" for biological evolution – or any evidence at all.

5.5 Psychologist Nicholas Humphrey

My father and I often talk about the wonders of the universe and the immense complexity of it all, especially life on Earth. We jokingly claim that the universe is really too complicated to actually exist and therefore the whole thing is a grand illusion. We call this absurd claim the Howell Hypothesis.

Imagine my surprise when I saw a genuine proposal akin to the Howell Hypothesis offered by a learned psychologist in *Intelligent Thought*. In the book, Nicholas Humphrey argues that consciousness is an illusion. He writes: "This challenge to consciousness's ontological status may dismay us, but should not surprise us. We can, and regularly do, have the experience of being in the presence of things that don't really exist: ghosts, for example, or mirages... Such illusions are accidental errors of judgment." He goes on to ask, "Is it plausible to suppose that our experience of consciousness is likewise some kind of *accidental* error? Since it is the wonderfully enigmatic features of consciousness that strike us so forcibly when we reflect on it, then perhaps it is those very features that give consciousness its role in life. And if that's the case, consciousness could have come to have these features not by accident, but because it has been *designed to give the impression of having them* – designed by natural selection, that is. So, while our experience is indeed an error, it is one for which we have been 'deliberately set up.'" (Emphasis in original).

This is the ultimate denial of reality. If consciousness is an illusion, then for all we know the whole of reality is an illusion. *You're not really conscious*, Humphrey whispers like a hypnotist. *It's all an illusion*.

This sort of denial of reality is the very definition of delusion. Despite the claims of Richard Dawkins, it seems that Dawkins and Humphrey are the deluded ones. Unfortunately, this brand of evolution-driven, reality-denying delusion is on the rise.

Although it was published in 1957, Humphrey seems to have missed the prophetic analysis of his illogical reasoning by John Galt in Ayn Rand's epic novel *Atlas Shrugged*:

> *"We know that we know nothing," they chatter, [ignoring] the fact that they are claiming knowledge – "There are no absolutes," they chatter, [ignoring] the fact that they are uttering an absolute – "You cannot prove that you exist or that you're conscious," they chatter, [ignoring] the fact that proof presupposes existence, consciousness and a complex chain of knowledge: the existence of something to know, of a consciousness able to know it, and of a knowledge that has learned to distinguish between such concepts as the proved and the unproved."*

After discussing the social benefits of religion, Humphrey concludes his essay with this: "So, here's the irony. Belief in special creation will very likely encourage believers to lead biologically fitter lives. Thus one of the particular ways in which consciousness could have won out in evolution by natural selection could have been precisely by encouraging us to believe that we have *not* evolved by natural selection."

Well, then, may the biologically fittest survive.

5.6 Philosopher Richard DeWitt

Richard DeWitt, in *Worldviews: An Introduction to the History and Philosophy of Science*, expounds on the claim by some leading evolutionists that objective morality is also an illusion. Says DeWitt, "Our understanding of the evolutionary origins of morality have made it overwhelmingly likely that although we often have the distinct sense that our moral judgments are objective, they really are not." Those evolutionists argue that our moral sentiments are as they are because they provided an evolutionary advantage, and not because our moral sentiments reflect an objective feature of the world and certainly not because they reflect the character of God.

However, these writers argue, our feeling that morality is objective is crucial to morality performing the evolutionary task that it does. That is, the apparent objectivity of moral judgments is a crucial component of morality. The sense of moral outrage we feel when we hear of cases of murder, rape, child abuse, and the like, the sense that the action really is wrong... is crucial to the evolutionary role morality plays. DeWitt continues: "We can now see, from understanding the evolutionary origins of our moral sentiments, that this sense of objectivity is an illusion. It is an important illusion, granted, and *not one that disappears once it is pointed out*, but an illusion nonetheless." (Emphasis added). In other words: I am telling you that your sense of morality is not objective, and if you think my assertion is manifestly ludicrous, trust me, not yourself.

Based on the conclusions of Humphrey and DeWitt, one might think biological evolution is very deceptive. I agree that it is, but not in the same sense as Humphrey and DeWitt. First consciousness is an illusion, now objective morality is an illusion. Apparently, all of life is just an illusion. And despite the evidence before their eyes, evolutionists must keep telling themselves (and us and our children) that they are right, and we are wrong. In the words of Francis Crick, co-discover of the structure of DNA, "Biologists must constantly keep in mind that what they see was not designed, but rather evolved." They must constantly keep it in mind because DNA – like consciousness and morality – unrelentingly screams CREATED. I am again reminded of Romans 1:18-20:

> *"For the wrath of God is revealed from heaven against all ungodliness and unrighteousness of men, who by their unrighteousness suppress the truth. For what can be known about God is plain to them, because God has shown it to them. For his invisible attributes, namely, his eternal power and divine nature, have been clearly perceived, ever since the creation of the world, in the things that have been made. So they are without excuse."*

DeWitt states authoritatively: "Morality stems from human nature, and our nature is as it is because of our evolutionary past." That is the only conclusion for an atheist. It is what it is because it just is. Or, it's all a grand illusion! However, for those holding a theistic worldview, morality stems from God's nature not human nature. *If* there really is a God, then morality really is objective. As Humphrey and DeWitt and the rest of Romans 1 illustrate, to deny the existence of God and objective morality is to fall a long way down the rabbit hole.

> *"For although they knew God, they neither glorified him as God nor gave thanks to him, but their thinking became futile and their*

foolish hearts were darkened. Although they claimed to be wise, they became fools and exchanged the glory of the immortal God for images made to look like a mortal human being and birds and animals and reptiles.

Therefore, God gave them over in the sinful desires of their hearts to sexual impurity for the degrading of their bodies with one another.

They exchanged the truth about God for a lie, and worshipped and served created things rather than the Creator – who is forever praised. Amen.

Because of this, God gave them over to shameful lusts. Even their women exchanged natural sexual relations for unnatural ones. In the same way, the men also abandoned natural relations with women and were inflamed with lust for one another. Men committed shameful acts with other men and received in themselves the due penalty for their error.

Furthermore, just as they did not think it worthwhile to retain the knowledge of God, so God gave them over to a depraved mind, so that they do what ought not to be done. They have become filled with every kind of wickedness, evil, greed and depravity. They are full of envy, murder, strife, deceit and malice. They are gossips, slanderers, God-haters, insolent, arrogant and boastful; they invent ways of doing evil; they disobey their parents; they have no understanding, no fidelity, no love, no mercy. Although they know God's righteous decree that those who do such things deserve death, they not only continue to do these very things but also approve of those who practice them."

DeWitt is not the only Darwinian philosopher who finds morality an illusion. In 2003, Alex Rosenberg of Duke University co-authored the paper[98] "Darwin's Nihilistic Idea: Evolution and the Meaninglessness of Life" in which he expounded on the idea. Almost ten years later, in a 2012 interview, Rosenberg declared that "conscious introspection was shaped by natural selection into tricking us about the nature of reality [that God and morality exist]."[99] Likewise, professor of philosophy Michael Ruse has declared that morality is an illusion fashioned by natural selection, but that fact doesn't diminish its usefulness or comfort.[100] Here again, evolution appears to be a master deceiver.

5.7 Conclusions Drawn From Non-biologists

Strictly speaking, evolution is a story about how biological organisms change over time – a creation myth describing the origins of humanity. In a broader sense, Darwinism is a worldview, a filter through which one sees the world and interprets what is seen. It is this "logic of Darwinism" that leads physicists to create mythological chronicles of reproducing universes spawning genetically-alterable offspring and leads philosophers on fanciful quests for the origin and meaning of natural and moral laws. This worldview is all-encompassing, as all worldviews are, and so it is this "logic of Darwinism" that creeps into airplane museum brochures. But I think that most reasonable people can see that when you follow this worldview all the way through to its remotest conclusions it becomes completely ludicrous, to the point of superstitious.

One theme continually emerges from the "logic of Darwinism," especially from non-biologists: the theory of evolution promotes a self-deprecating view of humanity. While most professional scientists avoid this sort of talk, non-biologists and amateur devotees of Darwinism seem to relish putting down the human race.

By way of example, bytesizebio.net published a review of a 2011 research article in which scientists sought the genes that make us human. The review began with a human-edifying quote by William Hazlitt: "Man is the only animal that laughs and weeps, for he is the only animal that is struck with the difference between how things are and how they ought to be." As it turns out, the quote was merely a straw man set up to be torn down. In the review, author Douglas Adams mocks that quote and ends with this: "Far out in the uncharted back waters of the unfashionable end of the western spiral arm of the galaxy lies a small unregarded yellow sun. Orbiting this at a distance of roughly ninety-eight million miles is an utterly insignificant little blue-green planet whose ape-descended life forms are so amazingly primitive that they still think digital watches are a pretty neat idea." Of course, his commentary begs the questions: Unfashionable to whom? Unregarded by whom? Insignificant to whom? Primitive compared to whom? And finally, are *not* digital watches pretty neat?

Certainly not every evolutionist holds such a loathsome view of humanity, but the opinion is nonetheless commonplace among them. Despite the prevalence of this attitude among lay evolutionists, professional scientists, if they say anything about humanity's worth, often posit the opposite viewpoint. I've already shared Brian Cox's feel-good sentiments he derives from the "scientific creation story." In a similar vein, Neil Shubin ends chapter two of *Your Inner Fish* with an unusual question: "Do the facts of our ancient history mean that humans are not special or unique among living creatures?" He answers the question, "Of course not." I am left curious, however, as to why he would pose such a question in the first place? Why would a biologist writing a book on evolution ask such a blatantly philosophical question? The answer seems obvious enough: Shubin understands the deeper philosophical implications of Darwin's theory – that God either does not exist or is irrelevant. Because he knows this point is not lost on those who believe there is a Higher Power, he must reassure his readers that humans *are* special and unique despite the fact, or *because* of the fact, that everything he said in the pages prior indicates otherwise. Further, Shubin does not explain *how* humans are special or unique and his silence there is also not lost on critical readers.

In his book *Worldviews*, Richard DeWitt continues the theme: "There seems to be a common belief that the evolutionary account forces on us some sort of dismal, less interesting view of the universe and our place in it. But the evolutionary account need not be taken in any sort of negative light. Evolution forces us to view our place in the big scheme of things in a very different way. But not, I think, in a worse way."

As one final example, I give you the Scientific American article "Why Life Does Not Really Exist" by science writer Ferris Jabr.[101] Recall that Nicholas Humphrey claimed consciousness is an illusion, and Richard DeWitt claimed objective morality is an illusion. Going a step farther, Jabr seriously proposes that life itself is an illusion. Life, according to Jabr, is a phenomenon that only exists in the human mind. He defends his position by pointing out that *life* is seemingly impossible to define.[102] Jabr is right that defining life is much more difficult than one would first imagine. Indeed, Jabr notes that biology textbooks don't even try to define life, rather they provide a list of attributes shared by living things: complexity, growth and development, metabolism, homeostasis, reaction to stimuli, and reproduction.[103] Jabr, however, finds this list – and any list – impotent to truly separate the living from the non-living. He asks: "Why is defining life so frustratingly difficult? Why have scientists and philosphers failed for centuries to find a specific physical property or set of properties that clearly separates the living from the inanimate?"

My answer: because you are seeking a *physical property* to define what is not physical.

God makes it very clear in the Scriptures that we (and He) are spiritual beings, that the physical body merely houses the actual person. After making Adam from the inanimate dust of the Earth, God breathed life into him. Jabr realizes that the physical property he's looking for doesn't exist, but he falls short of acknowledging the spiritual. *His* answer to his question: "Because such a property does not exist. Life is a concept that we invented."

Jabr sees our distinction between the living and the non-living as a line we draw at "an arbitrary level of complexity." He reiterates this conclusion when he writes: "What differentiates molecules of water, rocks, and silverware from cats, people and other living things is not 'life,' but complexity." Interestingly, he doesn't explain why a cat might be alive one moment and dead just seconds later. Certainly, the arrangement of its molecules and the level of its complexity hasn't slipped dramatically in those seconds. Clearly, Jabr's conclusion is just as ridiculous as Humphrey's and DeWitt's, yet this is where an aimless, purposeless Darwinian view of life takes you. Right on cue, however, Jabr finishes his article with the reassurance that we are still special. "Recognizing life as a concept," he declares, "in no way robs what we call life of its splendor." But like Humphrey, Shubin, Cox, and DeWitt, Jabr provides no clue as to what exactly makes us so splendid.

It should be evident by now that Darwinism is not just a theory of how biological species arise, it is a way of thinking. As we've seen, the "logic of Darwinism" has moved beyond biology to physics, philosophy, and even airplane brochures. Unfortunately, it is also seeping into medicine, a branch of science that has until recently avoided the Darwinian fray. It is becoming increasingly common to see references to evolution in medical literature. As one example, here is an excerpt of a description of pulmonary blood pressure provided by PathwayMedicine.org:

> "At normal pulmonary arterial pressures many pulmonary capillaries are either closed or only semi-patent. However, when arterial pressures rise, these pulmonary capillaries open or further increase in diameter, thus drastically reducing pulmonary vascular resistance

and thus preventing increases in the pulmonary blood pressure.
***Evolutionarily**, the low pressures within the pulmonary circulation
can be explained by considering that the maximum height which
blood must reach in the pulmonary circulation is only a few centime-
ters, that is, to the lung apex. Because low arterial pressures are
sufficient to perfuse these apical regions, the cardiac oxygen demand of the right heart is rendered quite low, thus allowing for significant energy conservation." (Emphasis added).*

The adverb "evolutionarily" is thrown in seemingly at random. The function, not the origin, of the pulmonary cardiovascular system is the topic of
discussion. If an adverb for *explained* is desired at all, *functionally* or *physically* would have been more appropriate since gravity is the implied force
that demands high arterial pressures. I cannot speak on why "evolutionarily"
was chosen by the author; however, bringing up evolution is both irrelevant
and unhelpful in this context. I can only conclude that it's a comfort word or
a signal that the author is part of the Darwinian club.

5.8 The Tone Used by Darwinists

The way evolutionists speak and write needs to also be addressed. I have
already pointed out several instances in which even the most speculative
and hypothetical notions have been presented as solid and indisputable
fact. In Section 3.3.8.3, I was quite critical of *Biology 10th edition*, yet the
authors of that text make as good as any attempt I've seen at being personally detached and impartial. I suspect, however, that the authors were being
more sanctimonious than sincere. Words like *possibly* and *perhaps* do little
to dampen the certainty of their conclusion: "At some point, life evolved."
Quite simply, this is not a statement of fact; it is a belief. A belief the teacher
intends for the pupil to accept even without supporting data.

More commonly, feeble attempts at impartiality are excluded entirely.
No doubt, the most ardent defenders of evolution speak so declaratively
because they so deeply believe in the concept. Although so much of their
talk is so manifestly derived from imagination, they can no longer discern
fact from fiction. Thornhill presents without reservation (as equally without
supporting evidence): "In the ancestral species in which primordial mammary glands arose, sweat glands were the typical end results of a particular

developmental process." Brian Cox boldly asserts that the LHC is a time machine that allows us to go "back in time" and "look into the past." Lee Smolin insists "there is indeed a multiverse consisting of a population of universes that are related to one another genetically." And if I choose to say, "No. I don't believe your creation story," then I am the one derided as an anti-science, knuckle-dragging baboon (which is quite ironic evolutionarily; Figure 5-1).

So be it.

5.9 The Switch

Evolution scientists often propose hypotheses, or conjectures, which are subsequently treated without confirming evidence as facts from which new hypotheses are advanced. The original hypotheses, never tested or confirmed, simply become the now-given foundational material upon which the next tale is spun.

Nicholas Humphrey performs the switch in a mere two sentences when discussing the origin of consciousness. "Consciousness *could have* [speculation] come to have these features not by accident, but because it has been designed to give the impression of having them – designed by natural selection, that is. So, while our experience *is indeed* an error, *it is* [solid fact] one for which we have been deliberately set up." (Emphases added).

To find another example of Darwinists spinning tall tales and treating them as fact, I randomly selected an evolution book from my university's

Figure 5-1: Creationists are depicted as evolutionary throwbacks.

library. The lucky book was *Finding Our Tongues* by Dean Falk. I didn't have to look any further than the preface to find all I was seeking.

Falk's entire thesis rests on 1) the assumption that today's baby-talk (or, *motherese*) existed millions of years ago and formed the basis of an assumed protolanguage (a unique twist on phylogenetic capitulation), and 2) the assumption that evolving to an upright posture led to the birth of premature babies that needed motherese for comfort (and survival). Says Falk:

> "Fossils show that an evolutionary dilemma arose when our ancestors began walking on two legs. The narrowing of birth canals associated with upright walking made giving birth excruciating and dangerous. As so often happens, this dire situation was solved by an evolutionary balancing act: only the smaller, less-developed infants (and the mothers of these smaller infants) survived the ordeals of birth. Because of their physical immaturity, these newborns lacked the ability to cling unsupported to their mothers, a skill that monkey and ape infants very quickly develop. Before the invention of baby slings, women would have had little choice but to carry their helpless babies on their hips or in their arms. More important, they would have been forced to put their infants down as they gathered food.
>
> When separated from their mothers, no doubt the babies fussed, as they do today, and busy prehistoric moms would have tried to soothe them. These mother-infant interactions began a sequence of events that led to our ancestors' earliest words and, later, the emergence of protolanguage."[104]

Serious question: do you detect *any* science in the above quote? Dr. Falk has a PhD and has published numerous books and articles in peer-reviewed journals. She is an accomplished scientist. Yet there is nothing – absolutely nothing – scientific about the tale just spun by this authority figure on the evolution of human speech. It is beyond speculation; it is fiction. The entire hypothesis is based on the premise that the human female pelvis got narrower when humans began walking upright, and this change led to premature births. However, there's no evidence for this assertion, which is treated as (i.e., *switched* to) an obvious fact for the rest of her book. Indeed, it is simple to find disconfirming evidence.

The size of the human birth canal is limited by the pelvic bones, specifically the pelvic diameters and conjugates (the minimal width and depth).

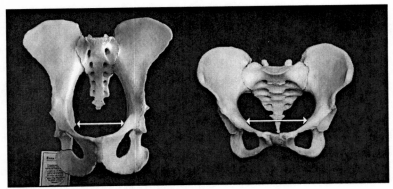

Figure 5-2: Human vs ape pelvis.

For a typical 5'5" 120 lbs. woman, these pelvic measurements are approximately 10 cm wide and 11 cm deep. Since Liberty University's Creation Hall has both a modern human skeleton and a modern ape skeleton on display, I decided to measure their pelvic bones. The human pelvis was approximately 10.5 cm wide and 11.5 cm deep, close to the expected values. The ape pelvis was roughly 8.5 cm wide by 11.5 cm deep.[105] Just by glancing at the pelvic bones in Figure 5-2 it is apparent that the birth canal in the human pelvis is *not* narrower than the birth canal in the chimp pelvis. This is objective fact. This is correspondent truth. Unfortunately for Dr. Falk, these measurements do not fit her narrative. Her story appears to be based on made-up conceptual facts that are merely coherent with her worldview and expectations, not reality.

---

[93] http://blog.godreports.com/2016/02/number-of-scientists-who-believe-in-god-remains-high-a-study-says/

[94] https://www.youtube.com/watch?v=wupToqz1e2g

[95] The Scopes Monkey Trial refers to the 1925 case against John Scopes, a schoolteacher charged with violating Tennessee's Butler Act which prohibited the teaching of evolution in Tennessee schools. Although legally a loss for Mr. Scopes, the highly public trial, regarded by most as a publicity stunt, was hugely successful for Darwinists who mocked and belittled creationists and greatly advanced the misunderstanding at the heart of this book: *evolution is science, creationism is religion.*

[96] https://www.youtube.com/watch?v=_6uKZWnJLCM

[97] Keim, B. 2010.How Darwin's Finches Keep Their Species Separate. http://www.wired.com/wiredscience/2010/11/darwin-finch-speciation/ (Accessed March 2017).

[98] Sommers, T. and A. Rosenberg. 2003. Darwin's nihilistic idea: evolution and the meaninglessness of life. *Biology and Philosophy* 18(5):653-668.

[99] http://blog.talkingphilosophy.com/?p=4209 [Accessed June 2016].

[100] Ruse, M. 2010. God is Dead. Long Live Morality. https://www.theguardian.com/commentisfree/belief/2010/mar/15/morality-evolution-philosophy [Accessed January 2017].

[101] Jabr, F. 2013. Why Life Does Not Really Exist. Scientific American blog. http://blogs.scientificamerican.com/brainwaves/2013/12/02/why-life-does-not-really-exist/ [Accessed January 2017].

[102] Here I would like to offer my own definition of life: *Living things are those entities which, through a constant influx of energy and a collection of chemical reactions called metabolism, are able to create order from disorder within themselves and maintain homeostasis.* Note that the 2nd Law of Thermodynamics is not violated because the overall disorder of the environment is increased ultimately by the burning of the sun.

[103] Jabr's list includes "ability to evolve."

[104] Falk, D. 2009. *Finding Our Tongues: Mothers, Infants, and the Origin of Language.* Basic Books.

[105] Technical details: the width of each pelvis was measured as the distance between the ischial spines (i.e., interspinous distance). The anteroposterior depth was determined at the narrowest point for each pelvis. In the human female pelvis, this was taken as the anatomical conjugate, i.e., the distance from the sacral promontory to the posterosuperior margin of the pubic symphysis. In the ape female pelvis, this distance was from the coccyx to the posteroinferior margin of the pubic symphysis. The pelvises were obtained from BoneClones.®

Epilogue

"A rat is a pig is a dog is a boy."
Ingrid Newkirk, President of PETA

Darwinism vs Christianity

"Evolution is science, creationism is religion." This is a falsehood being promulgated by scientists, teachers, judges, and other experts we rely on to accurately inform us on such things. In truth, divine creation and evolution are the creation myths of two competing and mutually-exclusive worldviews. It appears self-evident to me that our universe, the Earth, and all life upon it are the products of an intelligent mind. When we see the products of human ingenuity and recognize similar ingenuity in Nature, we don't have to "constantly remind ourselves that what we see evolved" as Francis Crick admonished. We can acknowledge that they are designed and have a Designer. We don't have to search endlessly for missing links when Nature's record of fossils already agrees with the Scriptures that God created each organism "according to its kind." Nor do we have to imagine unlimited variability in those fixed kinds in the face of limits imposed by developmental pathways and revealed by artificial breeding. We don't have to faithfully repeat a conclusion that flies in the face of our own findings, as Tompa and Rose did after essentially proving that life cannot arise spontaneously from chaos. And we find the observation that all mutations are negative consistent with the revelation that all things were originally created good. The revealed truths of Scripture align perfectly with the hard-fought truths pried from Nature if our agenda is not to discredit or disbelieve the Scriptures. Creationism is consistent with observed reality. It is Darwinism that takes flights of fancy into genetically-related universes, denies the reality of consciousness, and tells us that we are designed by evolution to detect false design in nature and to attribute that design to a fictional deity.

Despite the fatal flaws in Darwinism, belief in biological evolution now dominates our culture. Not surprisingly, Christianity is declining in America. Indeed, Christianity is under attack. There are at least two fronts to this battle against Christianity. First, a blatant and unapologetic assault against believers by those who want to strip "In God We Trust" from our currency and force Christian business owners to support every ungodly agenda or shut their doors. Second, a more subtle and perhaps far more dangerous loss of correct theology by those who purport to be Christians. I get the sense that there is a mushrooming group of "Christians" who claim to follow Christ but reject the clear teachings of Scripture, often out of ignorance of those teachings and a ready acceptance of the secular culture's morality. I attribute this in no small measure to the constant drumbeat of Darwinism thrust upon our children. Even where biological evolution *per se* is not being forced upon them, the godless worldview that underpins universal evolutionism is being passed off as science in every public classroom in America. Remember that 2016 Pew survey finding? Nearly 50% of adults who left the church name science as a factor. But Darwinism is not science. It is a worldview, and biological evolution is the creation myth of that worldview just as the biblical creation account is the creation myth of the Judeo-Christian worldview. These myths are sincerely believed as true by those who hold them. Since they are mutually-exclusive, only one of them can be true. Natural selection, the purported mechanism of biological evolution, can be tested empirically and the preponderance of the evidence does not bode well for natural selection. As examples: there are real limits to variability in organisms, there are no beneficial mutations, most populations are not controlled by a struggle for limited resources, and there is no naturalistic explanation for the origin of information. A plain reading of the evidence reveals that natural selection is not the engine that drives evolution; it maintains biological stasis. Thus, the only facts in favor of evolution are conceptual / philosophical facts that support a worldview built on coherent truths. Accordingly, Darwinism cannot be falsified.

Rejecting Darwinism and understanding the solid reasons why it is to be rejected can go a long way towards helping us more closely align our beliefs and worldview with Scripture. In other words, it will help us be transformed by the renewing of our minds and have a closer walk with Jesus Christ.

Impossible to Prove

How things are is evident by scanning the newspaper. *How things ought to be* unfortunately encompasses a vast expanse of strong disagreement (hence, the *how things are*). However, it is the worldview of the non-Christians that leads to the myriad conflicts in the world. Christianity is a gospel of peace. The record of history is crystal clear: the Judeo-Christian culture is *the* culture that tolerates differences in people and celebrates the value of every individual. It is the culture from which universities and hospitals sprang. It is the culture in which science took root and grew. It is the culture that seeks to treat every man, woman, and child of any race, age, or ability – born or unborn – with dignity. Indeed, it has been said that the level of Christianity in a society can be measured by the way it treats its women and children. Many non-Christians vehemently disagree, but then they are the same non-Christians that are the primary source of conflict in the world. It is the irreligious that are deceived. They are the blind leading the blind. They *think* they are on the side of peace when they create conflict. They *think* they are enlightened by sinking into darkness. They even think they please God: "A time is coming when the one who kills you will think he's serving God." (John 16:2). They *think* that Christians are evil for opposing abortion, for example, because in their worldview this is an attack on women, when in truth the scourge of abortion destroys both woman and fetus. Undeniably, atrocities have been committed in the name of Christianity, but those acts were committed largely by non-Christians (and a few confused Christians), those who face God after death only to be told, "Depart from me. I never knew you." (Matthew 7:23). Undoubtedly, most of the atrocities attributed to Christianity are trumped up charges. This world is Satan's after all (2 Corinthians 4:4) and he misses no opportunity to malign the faithful in film, newspapers, and history books, not just science books.

I marvel that two people can reflect deeply on the nature of our world and come to such dramatically different conclusions about God. How is this possible? If logic is real, if rationality is absolute, how can this be?

Logic *is* real. And rationality *is* absolute. In the end, the atheist employs flawed logic, but the flaws are so subtle and the web of flaws so tangled that it sometimes seems impossible to decipher or even expose. Nonetheless, close inspection reveals them, and I hope I've revealed some in this book.

No man can prove – or disprove – the existence of God. As a believer, I must conclude that God designed it this way on purpose because accepting Him now depends on faith (which for some reason is highly prized in us by

God). It is fascinating that God did prove his own existence through the resurrection of Jesus (and others) from the dead, and yet most of humanity still rejects Him. But as Jesus himself prophesied: "If they do not listen to Moses and the Prophets, they will not be convinced even if someone rises from the dead." (Luke 16:31). He also admonished: "Enter through the narrow gate. For wide is the gate and broad is the road that leads to destruction, and many enter through it." (Matthew 7:13).

At bottom, Darwinism is a worldview that captivates those who reject God. In the words of the late Allan Alexander MacRae:

> "The vital question concerning evolution is this: do we believe in God's existence or not? If we do not believe in God's existence, there is no alternative except the theory of evolution, but it is a theory which is irrational, which is not supported by solid evidence, a theory which leads to nothing but belief that one is part of an irrational universe moving by pure accident no one knows where.
>
> "[Evolution] is, by its very nature, unprovable... It actually rests on the unexpressed assumption that God does not exist."

But what if He does?

The evolutionist is charged with an impossible task: attempting to explain the origin of our universe, the Earth, and all life by purely naturalistic means without invoking a Creator. To get a sense of the futility of this task, imagine trying to explain the origin and development of modern computers without invoking mankind, a purely naturalistic origin to CPUs, keyboards, monitors, RAM, etc. It is a fool's errand. Yet imagine a world in which virtually all engineers and teachers promulgate this falsehood and more than half of the general population believes them. The masses uncritically accept because they trust the experts, but the honest experts (e.g., Lewontin and Crick) confess they believe despite the evidence.

Why are Darwinists so dedicated to the false narrative of evolution? Because the overwhelming majority of them are atheists. In the words of their most famous spokesman, Richard Dawkins: "Charles Darwin made it possible to be an intellectually fulfilled atheist." For them to admit that biological evolution is a failed hypothesis is to admit that they have a Creator, that He has ownership rights over them, and that they are accountable to Him. It requires them to confess that their entire worldview is wrong and based on lies and deception. That is a big pill to swallow.

Darwinism vs Liberty

In The Federalist Papers, Alexander Hamilton wrote:

> "It seems to have been reserved to the people of this country... to decide the important question, whether societies of men are really capable or not of establishing good government by reflection and choice, or whether they are forever destined to depend for their political constitutions on accident and force."

The American experiment is unique because the United States were founded through "reflection and choice" rather than the whims of accident or the army of a strongman. That reflection was made possible and animated by the Judeo-Christian worldview. From this worldview springs the concepts of natural rights, self-evident truths, individual sovereignty, and true liberty; the recognition that every man is created equal because we are created in the image of God; that just governments (as opposed to unjust governments) are instituted among men by the consent of the governed for the purpose of protecting each person's individual, natural (i.e., God-given) rights. Besides eternal salvation, God has granted us in America another invaluable gift: political liberty on Earth in the here and now. It is our responsibility to preserve the blessing of liberty and pass it on to our children and grandchildren and even to export that liberty around the globe to those who thirst for it. This can only be done by preserving and spreading the Judeo-Christian worldview. Chelsen Vicari, the Evangelical Program Director for the Institute on Religion and Democracy, put it this way: "If America's evangelicals disengage from the public square and fail to engage the rising generation of Christian leaders, then we risk losing our public voice, then our religious liberty, then liberty altogether."[106] Of course, it isn't just evangelicals who should engage in this fight but Christians of all stripes.

Darwinism attacks and displaces the central tenets of the Judeo-Christian worldview: the acknowledgement that there is a God, that we are created in his image, that we have rights given to us by God that no man (or congress of men) can take away, that the created Earth was charged to our care by its Creator, and that each one of us is responsible before God for our own behavior, to name a few. With the loss of these principles comes the fall of individual sovereignty and dignity, individual property rights, and the freedom of conscience and association. In a word, liberty. Darwinism is not something Christians can blithely dismiss as the folly of a few academics in their Ivory Towers. It is the atheistic worldview empowered by the invention of its own creation myth. It's a worldview that now shapes our culture and thus every aspect of our lives. The Scriptures warn of a great delusion that sweeps the world in the last days (2 Thessalonians 2). I believe that Darwinism will be the underpinning of that delusion. We can only push back against this ideology when we know the fallacies upon which it stands. Only then can we pull back its deceptive veil. May this book give you the understanding – and with it, the courage – to stand up to Darwinism.

---

106 http://www.charismanews.com/opinion/48678-the-new-christian-left-is-twisting-the-gospel Accessed January 2017.

Romans Road to Salvation

1. All have sinned and fall short of the glory of God (Romans 3:23).

2. For the wages of sin is death, but the gift of God is eternal life in Christ Jesus our Lord. (Romans 6:23).

3. That if you confess with your mouth "Jesus is Lord," and believe in your heart that God raised him from the dead, you will be saved. (Romans 10:9).

4. For everyone who calls on the name of the Lord will be saved. (Romans 10:13)

5. Therefore, since we have been justified through faith, we have peace with God through our Lord Jesus Christ. (Romans 5:1).

Romans Road explained:
As mentioned briefly in Chapter 1, sometime after God created Adam and Eve, they were tempted by Satan to rebel (i.e., sin) against God. Sadly, they yielded to that temptation, as we all still do to this day, and the result was and is death. Death, as defined in the Bible, is separation from God because of sin. As the descendants of Adam and Eve, we "inherited" sin and the death that comes with it – both physical death and spiritual death.

About two thousand years after the sin of Adam and Eve, God called a man named Abraham to follow Him and birth a nation, later to be known as Israel. The people of Israel – the Jews – were God's chosen people. God declared that he would judge the world for sin, but that through Israel He would provide a savior for the entire world. His salvation would allow men to escape God's judgement and would destroy sin and death forever.

About two thousand years after birthing the nation of Israel, God fulfilled his promise of a savior born in the lineage of Abraham. Jesus was miraculously conceived in a virgin by the Holy Spirit of God and is thus the Son of God and the Son of Man – the second Adam. Because Jesus lived a sinless life and was fathered by God, he knew no sin and was not subject to death. However, he willingly died on a Roman cross to be a sacrifice for our sin. Through this act, Jesus made what has been called *the great exchange* – he took our sin and gave us his righteousness. Dozens of Old Testament prophecies described details of his life and crucifixion hundreds and even thousands of years before his birth.

God's final judgement of the world has not happened yet, but it will. We are now almost 2,000 years from the crucifixion of Jesus Christ and many believe his second coming is eminent. God has declared that – like it or not – every knee will bow to Jesus and every tongue will confess that Jesus is Lord (Romans 14:11). Thankfully, Jesus freely offers salvation to anyone and everyone who will take it. Receiving salvation is simple: you only need to recognize your sin, turn from it (i.e., repent), and trust in Jesus for your salvation. If you do this, God has promised to save you from coming judgement and death.

Today, pray to God and ask him to forgive you of your sin and to receive his salvation. Then tell someone what God has done for you! Join a church and read the Bible to grow in your knowledge of Jesus and your salvation. And let me know, too, so I can rejoice with you!

Daniel Howell
Twitter: @barefoot_prof

Index

natural rights, 174
naturalism, 21
Nelson, Gareth, 128
Newton, Isaac, 16, 20-22, 26, 78, 125
non sequitur, 82, 85
Nye, Bill, 16, 30, 31

O

Obergefell v Hodges, 16, 17
operational science, 26-28, 34-36, 44
opinion(s), 2, 18, 53, 81, 104, 106, 108, 109, 148, 162
oranges, 34
orchard, 42, 43, 149
origins, 1, 3, 7, 18, 19, 20, 21, 27, 39, 44, 55, 58, 61, 64, 66, 71, 84, 88, 89, 123, 127, 131, 152, 159, 160, 162
Owen, Richard, 81, 82, 127

P

Paley, William, 103-106, 109
paradigm, 38, 39, 43, 45, 50-53, 71, 86, 95, 119, 149
paradigm shift, 48, 50
Pasteur, Louis, 16, 78, 79
pelvic, 167, 168
pelvis, 167, 168
Pew survey, 3, 171
phenotype, 62, 138
photo 51, 37, 72, 152
Pigliucci, Massimo, 35
plumber, 2
poetic, 11, 12, 152
poetry, 11, 12
Pontius Pilate, 20, 44
Popper, Karl, 22, 24, 27, 34, 43, 112
predictions, 33-35, 40, 66, 67, 112, 114, 127, 147
primordial soup, 14, 66, 123, 126, 138, 165
progeria, 14, 19
propaganda, 22, 134
prophecies, 13, 25, 177
prophets, 159, 173

proton(s), 63, 70, 153, 154
proximal, 107, 121
pseudoscience, 22-24, 31, 34
Public Broadcasting Service, 111
public education, 57

R

Rand, Ayn, 159
Randall, Lisa, 157
Reagan, Ronald, 37
reinforcement, 43. 44
reproduce, 28, 78-82, 109, 126, 131, 139-141, 146-148, 155, 156
resources, 126, 146-148, 154, 171
resurrection, 173
revelation, 1, 7, 8, 24, 25, 58, 170
robust, 28, 71, 113
Romans, 14, 15, 17, 18, 50, 53, 160, 176, 177
Rose, George, 63-65, 70, 170
Rosenberg, Alex, 161
Russell, Bertrand, 55, 56
Russian doll, 97, 98

S

Sagan, Carl, 1, 152, 153
salvation, 3, 53, 174, 176, 177
savages, 2
Schleiden, Matthias, 78
Schulson, Michael, 31
Schwann, Theodor, 78
Scopes Monkey Trial, 153, 168
Scientific American, 22, 115, 163
scientific method, 18, 20-23, 27, 44, 71, 80
Scott, Eugenie, 13, 34, 62
serpent, 7
Shaw, George Bernard, 123
Shermer, Michael, 105, 109, 110
Shubin, Neil, 23, 24, 38, 43, 44, 81-83, 85, 86, 97, 98, 103-108, 126, 128, 145, 154, 163, 164
sin(s), 7, 14, 176, 177
sinful, 15, 17, 161
Smolin, Lee, 154-156, 166
soft tissue, 30, 48, 129